The Open University
Arts: A Second Level Course
Seventeenth-century England: A Changing Culture, 1618–1689

A Different World

Prepared for the course team by Christopher Hill and Kevin Wilson

The Open University Press

Cover Front: Detail from 'The Prospect of Cambridge' by David Loggan. First published in *Cantabrigia illustrata* . . . 1690 (Mansell Collection)
Back: Covent Garden piazza *c.* 1640 by Wenceslaus Hollar (Mansell Collection)

The Open University Press
Walton Hall, Milton Keynes
MK7 6AA

First published 1980

Designed by the Media Development Group of the Open University.

Printed in Great Britain by
Eyre & Spottiswoode Limited at Grosvenor Press, Portsmouth

ISBN 0 335 11035 5

This text forms part of an Open University course. The complete list of the course appears at the end of this text.

For general availability of supporting material referred to in this text, please write to Open University Educational Enterprises Ltd, 12 Cofferidge Close, Stony Stratford, Milton Keynes MK11 1BY, Great Britain.

Further information on Open University courses may be obtained from the Admissions Office, The Open University, P.O. Box 48, Walton Hall, Milton Keynes MK7 6AB.

1.1

Block 1 A Different World

Contents

Introduction to Block 1

Aims of Block 1

In Block 1 we have attempted to do the following:

1   To evoke in you a 'feeling' for seventeenth-century England by reflecting on the differences between life then and life now – differences that embrace assumptions and ways of thinking as well as living and working conditions.

2   To make you aware of the changing social and economic structure of seventeenth-century England.

3   To cause you to reflect on the place of England in seventeenth-century Europe.

4   To introduce you to key concepts and constructs such as puritanism; biblical precedent; court and country; the general crisis of the seventeenth century, which the course team use to explore the theme of a changing culture.

5   To raise questions and issues which are linked to material you will study in later parts of the course, for example, censorship; the status of women in society; representative institutions versus absolute monarchy; continental influence on English art and architecture.

Set books

We have made extensive use of the following set books in Block 1:

Ann Hughes (ed.) (1980) *Seventeenth-Century England: A Changing Culture*, Vol 1 *Primary Sources*, Ward Lock (referred to as the Anthology)

W. R. Owens (ed.) (1980) *Seventeenth-Century England: A Changing Culture*, Vol 2 *Modern Studies*, Ward Lock (referred to as the Reader)

Christopher Hill (revised edn, 1980) *The Century of Revolution*, Nelson (referred to as *C of R*)

You will find it helpful to read the whole of Part One of *C of R* (pp 1–91) before starting Block 1. At the very least we advise you to complete this reading before proceeding to Block 2.

Broadcasting

Television programme 1, *Title to the earth*

Television programme 2, *Proud, ambitious heaps*

Radio programme 1, *Women in the seventeenth century*, Part 1

The two television programmes relate to Block 1 as well as being directly linked to 'Architecture and Society' in Block 2. The programmes examine a wide range of housing types. They bring out contrasts in life styles ranging from the hovels of the poor to the richly decorated houses of gentry and courtier and include the small farms of the yeomanry as well as an ostentatious home of a newly rich landowner. This study of domestic buildings serves to illustrate the theme of social and economic change.

The radio programme introduces the theme of the position of women in seventeenth-century society. This theme crops up throughout the course and especially relates to 'Middleton's *Women Beware Women*: Puritanism and the Theatre' (Block 2), 'Milton's Pamphlets on Marriage and Divorce' (Block 7), and 'A Restoration Comedy: *The Man of Mode*' (Block 9).

A Different World From Ours

1 Introduction

In this section I want to suggest some of the many ways in which life in seventeenth-century England was different from life in England today. If you went for a trip to the Middle East or Central Africa, you would expect the scenery, the architecture, the social customs and the food as well as the language to be different. And you would realize that these differences had to be accepted if you were to understand the country you were visiting. If you could get a time machine to take you back to seventeenth-century England, you would find even greater differences, and you must be fully aware of these if you are to understand what you are looking at in this course. The language appears to be the same, but that poses another problem: the same words may describe quite different things. There was a Parliament in seventeenth-century England, and a King; as we shall see, their functions were very unlike those of Parliament and Queen in England today. There were people called Puritans, but most of them were not killjoys or prudes. Even quite ordinary words change their meaning. When Henry Vaughan sings 'How fair a prospect is a bright backside', he doesn't mean what I suspect you may have thought. He is saying that it is nice to have a garden behind the house.

Let us use our time machine to visit seventeenth-century England. What differences would you expect to find between England then and England now?

This is an exercise in the use of your imagination, in no sense a test of your knowledge. Obviously there can be no set answer to such a wide-ranging question. These are the points that occur to me. Don't be alarmed if my response differs substantially from yours.

First of all it is important to consider how differences in the physical and social environment would affect styles of living and ways of thinking. The vast majority of the population lives in the countryside; except for London, all towns are by our standards very small. They are mostly markets for distributing agricultural products. Almost all industries at this date are processing agricultural products – the clothing industry, the leather industry, brewing, etc. There are no factories, few shops in villages: most people depend on travelling pedlars for goods, and themselves tramp to the local market town on market day. There are no cheques, no paper money. Tradesmen have to carry bags of cash around with them – almost an incitement to highway robbery.

Most people live by a totally unmechanized agriculture. They depend on the weather to an extent that is difficult for us to grasp. If the harvest fails, many people starve, and most are undernourished. A large part of the population is probably undernourished even in a good harvest year. Epidemic diseases – plague, influenza – recur frequently; smallpox and syphilis ruin many faces. Though a few live on to a ripe old age, average expectation of life is about half what it is today, and for the poor less than that. As a result, the proportion of children and young people in the population is far higher than now, although young children and mothers in childbirth have an exceptionally high death rate. In London some houses of the well-to-do have piped water: elsewhere there is no running water; there are no flush toilets. There are few hospitals or doctors, no anaesthetics: most people have to put up with a great deal of unrelieved pain. (Passages from Josselin's Diary in the Anthology, extract 61, illustrate this point.) The only cure for toothache or a gangrened leg is a barber-surgeon with a pair of pincers or a saw. The mentally ill are often chained up, receiving no treatment except an occasional flogging: mad people are regarded as amusing.

Diet – very restricted by our standards – varies with the seasons. Meat becomes expensive in winter. There is no refrigeration; salt meat and lots of dried or salted fish are consumed. There are no potatoes, tea or coffee at prices ordinary people can afford: far more beer and cider are drunk per head of the population than in most modern societies. Drunkenness may have been as common among the lower classes as over-eating among the rich. White bread is for the well-to-do. The authorities tend to restrict brewing in a bad harvest year, because barley is the principal bread corn of the poor. Sugar is a luxury too, its consumption per head of the population at the beginning of the seventeenth century less than 1 per cent of what it is today. This did however mean that teeth were better than they are now.

People measure time by the sun and the seasons; by our standards they are 'unpunctual'. There is no electricity or gas for heating or lighting. The poor tend to go to bed when it is dark, since candles and even rushlights are expensive. There is no street lighting, except in the very biggest towns, so people are much more aware of the moon and stars. Because of this, and of their dependence on the weather and the seasons, they are prepared to attribute importance to the influence of the sun, moon and planets on everyday life. Astrologers tried to make a science out of such beliefs, which nearly everyone shared. This proved a great stimulus to the rise of modern astronomy: seamen navigated by the stars as they reached out to trade with the recently-discovered America or utilized the recently-discovered sea routes to Asia and northern Russia. (You will hear more about this in Television programme 6, *Navigation*.) The omnipresent darkness at night helped to preserve traditional beliefs in ghosts, hobgoblins, fairies, witches and the supernatural. The Elizabethan prayer book calls on God to protect us from 'things that go bump in the night'. The magical significance of moonlight in Shakespeare's *A Midsummer Night's Dream* is stressed by Arnold Kettle, as students who did A101 will remember.

It is a society of much more extreme class divisions than ours. Probably not much less than half the population are by our standards very poor indeed, dependent on charity at least in bad times. In *C of R* I quote a phrase frequently encountered in Quarter Sessions records: 'no goods: to be whipped'. That is, many persons for offences for which they might have been fined simply could not produce the money: so they were flogged instead. The alternative of going to prison as a punishment did not exist. Gentlemen could always pay, so they were traditionally immune from the corporal punishments – flogging, branding – which were daily inflicted on the lower orders. One of the things that most shocked public opinion about the rule of Archbishop Laud in the sixteen-thirties was that he had gentlemen flogged, put in the pillory, deprived of their ears; and Laud was only a merchant's son himself! (See Anthology, extracts 24–6; *C of R*, p 38.)

Moreover, a society in which divisions between classes were immediately visible. (See Radio programme 5.) Just as a clergyman or a soldier was identifiable by his clothes, so was a lawyer, an academic, a farmer, a craftsman, a labourer, a gentleman. A man of lower rank thus knew when he must give way to his superior, or take off his hat to him. These distinctions of apparel were not just a matter of convention; they were laid down by law. Sometimes practice diverged from theory; there are many complaints of yeomen's wives and daughters wearing the silk garments appropriate to their social betters. But this is only a recognition of the fact that some yeomen (and merchants) were getting as rich as some gentlemen. Fashions changed only for the upper class: clothes for the poorer sort were handed on from one generation to another. As you will see in Television programmes 1 and 2, the gentry lived in stone houses many of which have survived; the houses of the lower classes, built of timber, mud and clay, have not. So it is much more difficult to imagine how the latter lived. It is one of the many ways in which the survival of evidence biases our historical knowledge in favour of the upper classes.

In one sense of course the gentry (and rich merchants in towns) were, as they regarded themselves, the 'natural rulers' of the country: it is a phrase which we shall often meet. In any society the rich have more influence than the poor. But the discrepancy between the numbers of the 'natural rulers' and their influence was very marked in seventeenth-century England. In the 1690s Gregory King made estimates of the population and social structure of England which are still cited by demographers, if only because they have very little else. If we add together King's peers, bishops, baronets, knights, esquires, gentlemen, greater and lesser office-holders, merchants and traders by sea and land, lawyers – all those with incomes of more than £100 a year – they amount to only just over 3 per cent of the population. (See Anthology, extract 2.) Yet, except for the years 1640–60, it is normally the views of this tiny minority (and of the clergy whom they patronize) which get into print; our accounts of 'political disputes' in the country are in fact disputes within this minority who compose 'the political nation'. The other 97 per cent, in the classic words of General George Monck, 'have no interest in the commonwealth but the use of breath'. That is where most of us would have been in the seventeenth century. Similar sentiments expressed by one of Queen Elizabeth's Secretaries of State and by a Caroline baronet are quoted in *C of R* (pp 37–8). But, as we shall see later, from the beginning of our period some of 'the middling sort' were taking a quite novel interest in politics.

Seventeenth-century society was much more close-knit than ours. Many villages had a resident lord of the manor whose standard of living and style of life were vastly superior to those of the villagers. He was also likely to be the principal local employer of labour: the boss was very rarely a distant impersonal corporation, but a real person, whom one saw regularly, who went to the same church every Sunday, who was expected to distribute charity to the poor. Almost all communities, whether town or villages, were small: the impersonality and loneliness of life in large modern cities was known only in London. From Television programme 1 you may get an impression of families living in very isolated houses. This would be less true of the more densely populated South and East of England than of North Yorkshire with which this programme deals.

It was still a society in which opportunities were very unequal. If you were a gentleman's younger son who wanted to get on in the world, it helped to have a 'good lord' to give you a push. Children of gentry families went to serve in the household of a great aristocrat, in the hope of a job or a lucky marriage. If you were on the permanent staff of a lord as his 'retainer', you wore his 'livery' – his uniform as it were. It tells us a lot about the society and the church's place in it that clergymen under Elizabeth were described as 'wearing the Queen's livery'. Another phrase is also illuminating: 'God is a better lord than the Earl of Derby'. If you lived in Lancashire or the Isle of Man, it was difficult before the civil war to think that anyone could be more powerful than the Earl of Derby (and of course there were powerful if less omnipotent magnates in other regions in the first half of the century, though London was different). It would need great courage to stand up against your local lord. One of the features of Puritanism (which we shall be discussing later) is that it gave men this courage. If in a crisis you *really* believed that God was more powerful than the Earl of Derby and that he was on your side, this must have given an extraordinary confidence to normally diffident men. When enough of them believed it they could take on the whole social hierarchy, the King himself included.

Independent households predominated in the economy: families with their own holding (whether they were owner-occupiers or tenants) which they might supplement with other earnings. (We shall return to this point in Block 4, *The Revolution and its Impact*.) The family provided such social security as there was. No dole, of course, no sickness benefit, no paid holidays, no widows' or old age pensions, indeed no retirement except through incapacity: most men and women had to work just as long as they could. If the family would not or could not look after an able-bodied unemployed member, he or she probably took to the road, joining thousands of others in the elusive search for employment elsewhere. 'The impotent poor', meaning cripples and the aged, got 'poor relief' if they were permanent inhabitants of a parish; but this was a charity, not a right and was often doled out in barely adequate amounts. Pauper children were compulsorily apprenticed to masters who might or might not treat them well.

At least at the beginning of our period, money was more important for paying rent, tithes and taxes than for shopping (see p 16 below for tithes). A great many families grew their own food, made their own clothes, picked up fuel from the commons, or from the woods and forests of which there were far more than today, and which were a source of food too. That is why, as we shall see later, attempts to take commons or forests into private ownership by enclosing them could have disastrous consequences for the poor, even though the long-term effect was that they were cultivated and more food was grown. In order to pay rent, tithes and taxes, some members of some – perhaps most – peasant families had to work part-time in industry. This usually meant the women and children doing spinning or weaving at home for cloth merchants. So when there was a depression in the clothing industry – as there was when our period begins – it caused extreme hardship among thousands of families whose principal occupation was agriculture but who depended on industrial bye-earnings to make ends meet, just as today the budgets of many families can be balanced only by overtime, or by the wife going out to work, or both. During our period a money economy became increasingly important as more men and women lost their land, or access to land, and became wholly dependent on wage labour. They still needed the commons, wastes and forests to keep them alive during unemployment.

In seventeenth-century society there were no means of travel except on horseback for the fortunate and on foot for the rest. (Though of course Britain being an island, with many – then – navigable rivers, much of the country's trade was carried by water.) Carts were used locally and coaches were just beginning to be introduced, but only the very rich could afford them. (Clothiers complained that coaches would be their ruin: people's clothes would not wear out half so fast as if they travelled on horseback exposed to the elements and to the mud of the roads!) In Elizabeth's reign in the sixteenth century bishops used to visit their dioceses on horseback. From the reign of James I in the seventeenth century they travelled in coaches. At a time when 'lordly bishops' were increasingly unpopular, their being shut up in a coach seemed symbolic of their separation from their flock; as long as they rode on horseback they were on a level with any yeoman. So too the royal Court ceased to move round the countryside and settled permanently in and around London. The effect was to cut the King off from direct visual contact with his people.

In fact there was a surprising amount of mobility in seventeenth-century England. But it was largely a mobility of apprentices and servants, of the very poor looking for work, and of rogues and vagabonds who had given up the hope of ever finding work. Such persons were the product of over-population and of the agricultural changes of the sixteenth and seventeenth centuries – including enclosure of corn-growing land for sheep-farming, and the consequent eviction or voluntary removal of those for whom the parish no longer grew enough food; or of enclosure of the commons and wastes on which the poorer members of the community depended for many of the necessities of life.

If you look at Joan Thirsk in the Reader, article 7, you will see that she distinguishes sharply between docile peasants living in a corn-growing village under the eye of parson and squire, on the one hand, and on the other cottagers and squatters living in woods, fens and moors. This is not merely a distinction between pastoral North and West and agrarian South and East, though that is part of it. Even in the south-east there were far more forests, fens and wastes than it is easy to imagine today.

As their name suggests, cottagers – i.e. squatters, the shanty-town dwellers of their time – lived in appalling conditions in mud or wooden huts which they built themselves. Television programme 1 shows huts of this sort. Their inhabitants might be employed as casual labour in industry; or they would live off what they could gather from the woods or commons or could beg or steal. But Dr Thirsk also suggests advantages: such men had no landlord collecting rent, no parson collecting tithes. They could escape the obligation of going to church every Sunday. They could move on when they wanted to. They were 'masterless men', with no place in the hierarchy of agrarian society, no dependence. In their poverty they were in some ways freer than the poor husbandmen described by Richard Baxter (Anthology, extract 8). You will later be reading *The Pilgrim's Progress*, written by the tinker John Bunyan. It is in a sense the epic of the itinerant.

EXERCISE

Some historians suggest that daily familiarity with pain and death must have had a brutalizing effect on personal and family relationships. What do you think?

DISCUSSION

The assumption is that because so many children died in infancy, because so many marriages were dissolved early by the death of one of the partners, therefore affection between man and wife, and between parents and children, must have been less than today. I am sceptical of this myself. How does one know anyway? How does one measure affection? Not all marriages generate affection: it has been suggested that one reason why divorce is more common today is that people live longer. Ralph Josselin's name has already been mentioned. If you read the extracts from his Diary in your Anthology carefully, I think you will agree that they suggest no lack of parental affection, or insensitivity to the death of young children. There was indeed one man who in his will in 1629 left a relatively small sum to the wife whom he had recently married because, he said, 'I had her so little a while'; but I don't think we should generalize from him.

We can however perhaps speculate that daily familiarity with pain made the cruel punishments of the law – whipping, branding, hanging, disembowelling and quartering – seem less shockingly horrible than they do to us today. John Bunyan indeed spoke slightingly of 'those petty judgements among men, as putting in the stocks, whipping or burning in the hand'. His object however was to contrast such penalties with eternal torment in hell; and perhaps we may even think that the continuing belief that God had condemned the majority of mankind to an eternity of torture also seemed less frightful in seventeenth-century society. Many parsons believed that most men and women were so incurably sinful that only the fear of hell kept them from continual outrages: and if pain was familiar, the deterrent threat of hell had to be so much the greater.

Brutal punishments also relate to absence of prisons as places of punishment. Like the use of torture to obtain evidence in treason trials, they also relate to inadequacies of the police and legal system. There were no professional policemen. The King's peace was supposed to be maintained by members of each parish elected by their neighbours for a year's term of duty: they were, naturally, not always very assiduous in prosecuting those neighbours whom they would rejoin at the year's end. Communal arrangements covered, for instance, sanitation; it was tempting to empty chamber pots and the contents of earth closets into the streets, which were already foul from the domestic animals roaming about them. Maintenance of bridges and highways was the responsibility of the parish authority, so at the local level there was a good deal of self-government.

EXERCISE

In seventeenth-century England there were none of the media with which we are familiar – no radio, no television, no daily newspapers, no cinemas, no theatres outside London. Have a look at pp 63–4 of *C of R*. What do you think were the social consequences of living in such tight-knit communities?

DISCUSSION

I suggested that the parish church was the only community centre outside big towns, and that parsons were the only opinion-formers. This changed in some areas as political tension grew in the late 1630s. In Colchester, Thomas Cotton used to read intelligencers' news in the streets on market days to listeners crowding round 'as people use where ballads are sung' (Hunt, *The Puritan Moment*). Perhaps I should have added to the parish church the ale-house as the community centre of the poor. Footloose vagabonds wandering the country in search of work would go first to the ale-house on entering a new village. That is why ale-houses were something which the local gentry as Justices of the Peace insisted on keeping under their control. In towns first taverns and later coffee-houses provided social centres for the well-to-do. When normal controls broke down in the 1640s, radical religious or political groups – Baptists, Levellers, Ranters – used to meet in London taverns. Charles II's government was highly suspicious of coffee-houses as places in which sedition might be discussed.

I should also have made more in *C of R* of the growing importance of the home, the household, for the middling sort. In the South and East of England many of those peasant, merchant and artisan families which survived the economic crises of the sixteenth and early seventeenth centuries were prospering – building themselves houses made of stone instead of lath and plaster, adding an upper story to existing houses, putting in stairs, glass windows, better furniture, giving themselves greater comfort and privacy, the possibility of reading, of entertaining friends and neighbours. (Harrison elaborates this point – see Anthology, extract 3 – and it is illustrated in Television programme 1. Compare also the farm and cottage inventories, extract 6 in the Anthology. In the North and West this development came later; very few non-gentry houses survive from the early seventeenth century. In the North the church was often referred to as 'the stone house', presumably to distinguish it from all the other buildings in the village. Only with greater security and prosperity after the civil war was there an outburst of peasant and artisan building in stone in the North.

A household which had apprentices and servants living in as well as the immediate family became almost a separate community, in which the father – the head of the household – was responsible for the moral and religious education and technical training of his dependants. Remember there was no compulsory schooling. In some villages there were dame's schools; in others none. But for most of the population education was obtained on the job, either in the family or by apprenticeship into another household. This helps to account for the tendency of boys to follow their father's calling, which kept the society relatively static; the only refuge from family claustrophobia was to send a son or daughter away as an apprentice or servant to someone else's household. One may suspect that – as with the later upper-class habit of sending children away to boarding school – the object was at least as much to liberate parents from teenage children as to obtain a good education for the latter.

So it was a society in which culture was mainly transmitted orally. Village festivals and junketings still helped to hold communities together. Boys learnt their parents' craft skills, and took over inherited attitudes to morals, politics, society. It was thus a world resistant to change. Traditional songs and ballads, traditional proverbs and sayings, traditional weather-lore, traditional charms and spells; memories of the good old times. When we come to consider the political and religious ideas of the period, this should prepare us to understand why men looked to the past for guidance.

An oral society then with no accredited media, except the parson on Sunday; such books as were printed (before 1640) were submitted to clerical censorship. It was therefore a society which tended in moments of crisis to be at the mercy of rumours, panics, superstitions. We shall come across plenty of these later in the course. All this may prepare us to understand the extraordinary effect of the collapse of the censorship when it occurred after

1640. Printing itself was less than two centuries old; literacy had slowly advanced in the century after Henry VIII's reformation. But the press had never been free. What was printed was what the ruling authorities, especially the ecclesiastical authorities, saw no objection to. There were no printing presses outside London, Oxford and Cambridge. (This is discussed in *C of R*, pp 82–3.) In the 1640s all that suddenly changed. The London bookseller George Thomason listed 22 titles of books and pamphlets published in 1640, 1,966 in 1642. Printers were small craftsmen: little capital was needed to set up a press. There were consequently no press lords or big publishing firms. So for a few brief years almost anything could get into print. No wonder conservatives wanted to restore censorship as soon as they could.

The dominance of the household had its effect on political ideas. When men discussed the concept of authority in the early seventeenth century they almost invariably started from the fifth commandment, Honour thy father and thy mother. (See James I in the Anthology, extract 10.) Just as the head of the household ruled over and was responsible for the welfare of his family (including his employees), so the King was responsible for the various communities – counties, parishes, households – which formed his kingdom. There was not much need of political theory so long as this 'natural' hierarchy prevailed unchallenged. Even during the civil war it proved very difficult to escape from the deeply-held belief that if only the King's evil councillors were removed the King himself would rule the country well. The conviction that the gentry – the men with swords – *must* rule under the King could be shaken for the first time only when a lot of Englishmen who were not gentlemen also found themselves with swords in their hands. It is from the discussions of this period that modern political theory dates, modern ideas about authority. We shall be looking later at the Levellers, the first modern democratic political party: at Thomas Hobbes, from whom derive modern ideas of sovereignty and a rational-utilitarian approach to politics; at Gerrard Winstanley and James Harrington, both of whom believed that constitutions and politics must be influenced by economics and social structures. Winstanley was the first politician to appeal for lower-class support for a communist organization of society.

2 The position of women

Here is a story from a seventeenth-century jestbook. I apologize for its very sexist character, but that will perhaps tell you something about the society:

> Two persons who had been formerly acquainted, but had not seen each other a great while, meeting on the road, one asked the other how he did. He told him, he was very well, and was married since he saw him. The other replied, that was well indeed. 'Not so well neither', said he, 'for I have married a shrew', 'That's ill', said the other. 'Not so ill neither', said he, 'for I had £2,000 with her'. 'That's well again', said his friend. 'Not so well neither, for I laid it out in sheep, and they died of the rot'. 'That was ill indeed', said the other. 'Not so ill neither', said he, 'for I sold the skins for more money than the sheep cost'. 'That was well indeed', quoth his friend. 'Not so well neither,' said he, 'for I laid out my money in a house and it was burnt'. 'That's very ill', said the other. 'Not so ill neither', said he; 'for my wife was burnt in it'.

EXERCISE

What insights about seventeenth-century England can you get from that story?

DISCUSSION

Yes, it is a male-dominated society. But the jest also tells us some things about the economy. I stressed earlier men's dependence on the weather. This story underlines the fact that it was not yet possible to take out an insurance policy against the natural catastrophes which were so much more frequent then than now. Even when it had become possible, later in the century, an almanac writer suggested confidently that 'a little astrology . . . may prove more advantageous to you than your insurance officer'. Diseases of sheep and cattle were rife and unchecked; timber-built and thatched houses, lighted by candles or rushlights, with open coal and wood-burning fires, were terribly liable to fires (especially in the crowded towns, where fires once started were almost impossible to check: there were no fire-brigades. See Pepys's account of the Fire of London in the Anthology, extract 129). An accident could easily ruin a prosperous farmer: a piece of good luck might bring windfall profits. Ralph Josselin's Diary tells us how he lost his share when a ship was wrecked, and also of a poor man whose house was burnt down. His neighbours collected £3 for him – a nice gesture, but it cannot have paid for rebuilding the house. Josselin reflected deeply on the explanation of such misfortunes, on how the sins of individuals and of the nation provoked God's judgements (Anthology, extract 61). (Later we may speculate about connections between this background of economic insecurity and Calvinist doctrines of predestination – those who were fortunate enough to be saved owed it to the grace of God, not to their own merits.)

But the story makes another point. The train of events was set in motion by marriage, for the wife brought capital; and at the end the husband is free to look around for another well-endowed wife and start again. For the propertied class marriage was an economic transaction: a good dowry could be more important than good looks or a good disposition. It might be greatly to the disadvantage of a landowner with social aspirations to have too many daughters. Those with no property were at least freer to choose their partners. You will hear more about marriage and the position of women in Radio programme 1. Here, since we are dealing with the differences between the seventeenth and twentieth centuries, it is important to stress two points. First, the law and orthodox theology assume that women are inferior to men. Milton's notorious remark that Adam and Eve were created 'He for God only, she for God in him' expressed a seventeenth-century commonplace; indeed many of his contemporaries thought Milton too favourable to women. But, secondly, as one commentator put it, after stating that 'a wife in England is *de jure* [in law] but the best of servants, having nothing in a more proper sense than a child hath, . . . their condition *de facto* [in fact] is the best in the world, such is the good nature of Englishmen toward their wives'. We may come to think of other explanations than the virtues of English men, but the fact is correctly reported.

The relatively favoured status of wives in England was related to the changing economic structure. The household was the principal productive unit, and although the father as head of the household was deemed to have authority over wife, children, apprentices, servants, still his wife was the No. 2 in the firm and had a good deal of delegated authority. Wives stood in for their husbands when they were absent (on business, or at the wars in the 1640s); and widows often continued to run their late husband's business. The development of bye-industries also enabled unmarried women to earn. It is just at this period that the word 'spinster' acquires its modern meaning: it was assumed that any unmarried women would spin yarn.

In these circumstances marriage for 'the middling sort' of people was a serious economic step. It meant setting up one's own household, and the choice of a suitable partner for the firm was an important one. So economic developments supported a new ethic of marriage, which is sometimes called 'Puritan', though it started before the Reformation, and something similar is to be found in Roman Catholic countries too. But Puritans, whose ideas appealed especially to 'the middling sort', were its main exponents in

England. This ethic stressed the importance of matrimonial fidelity and of loving one's partner. Marriages should not be arranged for children by their parents (as they traditionally were among the propertied classes); young people should have some choice in the matter. This became especially important since the age of marriage was very late – 27–8 for men of all but the highest social class, 24–5 for women (see Stone in the Reader, article 1). On the other hand the rather free-and-easy attitude towards separation and divorce, which seems to have been common among the unpropertied classes, was frowned on. Milton was to argue that if you married for love, then total incompatibility should be a reason for divorce. But this view seemed outrageous to the orthodox, and proved acceptable only among some of the more radical sects. Children, for the vast majority of the population, were an economic liability for the first few years, but additions to the family work force from the age of 6 or 7. Formal education for children of the poor consequently never got very far. One can imagine the strains which would exist in a family where teenage children were expected to work for their parents, and where the authority of the father was theoretically very great. This was mitigated in many ways – first by the habit of sending children out as servants and apprentices to other families, secondly by the practice of consulting children's wishes, so that the theoretical absolutism of the father often became a sort of limited monarchy. But we do not know enough about the proportion of families in which government was by consent. In Block 5, *Political Ideas*, you will be looking at patriarchal theories of monarchy, of which Sir Robert Filmer's is the best known. They arose naturally in this patriarchal society.

One of our perennial problems indeed is our ignorance of how ordinary people lived. As in the case of buildings, the surviving evidence tends to be class-biased. It is also often sex-biased. It is absurd that we should have to treat one half of the population – women – as a subject requiring special research. But the male domination of seventeenth-century society prevents our understanding their lives or hearing their point of view without making a very deliberate effort.

3 The metropolis

I have said little about London so far, and that is right in a sense, since 90 per cent of the population lived outside the capital. Nevertheless, London was the engine that drove England. It was not only the seat of the Court and government, it was also the centre of a rapidly expanding home and foreign trade, and of the country's intellectual life. Oxford and Cambridge trained parsons, and many sons of gentlemen spent a year or two there. But the most ambitious of the parsons whom they trained hoped for a living or a job in London, and aspiring gentlemen flocked to Court if they could, or strove to represent their counties in the House of Commons when a Parliament was summoned.

London was described as England's 'third university'. Lawyers – increasingly important in a society in which litigation was replacing private war – were trained there; the Inns of Court were also finishing schools for the sons of the gentry. Men who wanted to learn mathematics, essential for such important activities as sailing ships and surveying lands, had to come to London. Above all London was the centre of a unique literary culture. Nowhere else in Europe was there a popular commercial theatre like that for which Shakespeare had written, and for which Ben Jonson, Beaumont and Fletcher, Middleton, Webster and Dekker were still writing when our period begins. Aspirant writers came to London, hoping for a patron or a lucky break into the theatre. The unemployed flocked to London too, where they were housed in slum squalor looking for casual jobs. In London ordinary people could live free from supervision by landlords and parsons: the anonymity of city life must have been one of its main attractions for the much-supervised lower classes. London's crowded state alarmed early Stuart governments: plague in 1625 and 1636, popular tumults in and after 1640, show how right they were to want to control it.

Compared with the metropolis, other towns were very small. Even London, at the beginning of our period, was comparable in size to Leicester today, with perhaps 200,000 inhabitants – 5 per cent of a total population of some 4 million for England and Wales. (Today it is 52 million.) Another 120,000 or so lived in 17 or 18 towns with over 5,000 inhabitants; apart from London, only Norwich, York and Bristol had more than 10,000. (All seventeenth-century population figures are very tentative, since there was no census before 1801; historians have to use indirect evidence of various kinds in making their estimates.)

4 England or Britain?

Seventeenth-century Englishmen did not like foreigners, and one way in which their world differed from ours is that Scots and Irishmen were regarded as foreigners. Scotland and Ireland were separate kingdoms (except for a brief period in the 1650s when they were incorporated into England). Scotland was the 'auld ally' of England's traditional enemy, France. James I united the English and Scottish crowns, but Parliament defeated his attempt to unite the two kingdoms. His Scottish favourites were very unpopular. In the 1630s and '40s Scottish armies helped to defeat Charles I. But armies of occupation are seldom popular, and northern Englishmen were glad to see the backs of 'our brethren of Scotland'. Attitudes towards the Irish were less ambiguous. Englishmen conquered and ruthlessly exploited Ireland in the sixteenth and seventeenth centuries. They justified this by denouncing the Irish as culturally inferior – and papist to boot. Sensitive poets like Edmund Spenser and Sir John Davies wrote of the Irish in terms that might seem extreme to a defender of apartheid today; such unpleasant attitudes dominate English thinking about Ireland throughout our period.

In politics, administration, economics, religion and culture the histories of Scotland and Ireland are quite distinct from those of England. Only after our period ends was Ireland finally conquered, in William III's wars of the 1690s; only in 1707 was Scotland again united to England, and only after 1745 were the Highlands finally subdued. What happened in our period is very significant for explaining twentieth-century Scottish and Irish nationalism; but in the seventeenth century relations between England on the one hand and Scotland on the other are relations between quite different communities and cultures. The principality of Wales, on the other hand, had been united to England in 1536, and, despite considerable cultural differences, its development relates much more closely to that of England.

At the beginning of our work the course team discussed very carefully whether our subject should be 'seventeenth-century England' or 'seventeenth-century Britain'. We decided, reluctantly, that we must exclude Scotland and Ireland except in so far as those countries affected developments in England. This was not because we thought their histories unimportant: quite the contrary. But we felt that Scotland and Ireland were so different from England in the seventeenth century that to deal with them in any detail would have overburdened a course which some may feel already contains more than enough. It would be fascinating to study the changing cultures of Scotland and Ireland in the seventeenth century, and to compare and contrast them with England: we hope that somebody will tackle the subject some day. Meanwhile, we hope that Scottish and Irish students will accept our apologies!

5 Religion

Some people say that the seventeenth century was a more religious age than our own. I don't like that way of putting it, because no reliable instrument for measuring religiosity has, so far as I know, yet been invented. It could be argued that in many respects the seventeenth century was a *less* religious age than our own. The ways in which Englishmen treated their churches would shock a modern congregation. They wore hats, they smoked, they brawled, they scuffled for the best seats. Some gallants went 'only to see faces', a character in *Women Beware Women* tells us. Samuel Pepys, one sermon-time, took 'a pretty modest maid' by the hand and the body; she defended heself by sticking pins into him. Others brought their dogs in, with disastrous consequences. When that great traveller Fynes Moryson found himself in Turkey he noted as an eccentricity of the Moslems that they thought it wrong to spit in their mosques.

Take another example: all Englishmen were liable to pay tithes, nominally one-tenth of their produce or earnings, to the rector or vicar of their parish. These payments were enforceable in the law courts. Some people in the seventeenth century suggested that payment of tithes should be made voluntary. Others disagreed. But all agreed on one point – that if the parson could not take people to court to get his money, he would starve. Some thought that would be a good thing, others a bad thing; but all agreed on the facts. Whereas today, though church attendance is smaller than it was in the seventeenth century, far more than 9,000 clergymen (roughly the number of parishes in seventeenth-century England) are maintained by contributions which are for the most part voluntarily paid by congregations. This too would suggest that the seventeenth century was a *less* religious age than our own.

What is the fallacy in this argument? It is that we are comparing unlike things. In seventeenth-century England every man and woman was legally obliged to go to church every Sunday; those who did not could be fined. Today congregations (adults anyway) attend because they choose to. How decorous would church services be today if the whole population *had* to attend? Similarly with tithes. In the seventeenth century many well-to-do members of congregations did contribute generously, over and above their legal liability, to the maintenance of a favoured minister; it was the universal compulsion that was resented, and the fact that the poor and middling sort had no say in choosing ministers.

These two examples highlight a point made on pp 63–7 of *C of R*, that all Englishmen were members of the Church of England, whether they liked it or not. Officially everybody believed in Christianity. There were no doubt many people with a 'couldn't-care-less' attitude whom the godly described as atheists, but so far as we know there was little if any intellectually worked-out atheism. I say so far as we know, since anyone who proclaimed himself an atheist would have been in very serious trouble indeed; but before the rise of theories of evolution it would have been difficult to produce an intellectually satisfying explanation of the working of the universe that did not assume that it had been planned and created by God. God was believed to take a direct daily interest in the lives of everyone and of all communities: natural disasters – war, plague, famine – were much more frequent than in England today: more like the Third World. As Josselin's Diary shows, they were regarded as God's punishments for our sins, though of course men could argue about which sins had offended the deity.

The rivals to orthodox Christianity were either heresies or magical beliefs. The last Englishmen were burnt for heresy in 1612, six years before our period starts; but heretics were liable to severe punishment at least until 1640. Thomas Hobbes was afraid that the bishops would burn him after 1660 because of his 'irreligious' book, *Leviathan*; the statute authorizing the burning of heretics was not repealed until 1679. The last witch was executed in England in 1685, but at the beginning of our period most men almost cer-

tainly believed in witchcraft, and alleged witches were periodically perse-
cuted.

EXERCISE

Read Keith Thomas on witchcraft in the Reader, article 3 and ask yourself
what the causes and social consequences of belief in witchcraft were. Why do
you suppose persecution was acute in the early seventeenth century?

DISCUSSION

Keith Thomas suggests that increased persecution of witches may have
economic causes. A few villagers are getting richer, but the mass of the
peasantry are sinking into permanent poverty. Persecution of witches may
have been a product of guilt feelings among members of a village community who refused, or were no longer able to maintain, charity towards the
very poor, particularly widows, of whom there were always many in every
village. Traditional ideas of mutual interdependence were giving place to a
more individualistic conception of private property. The manorial structure
which had done something to provide for the poor was disintegrating; a
regular system of poor relief was in process of being established. In communities in Shropshire where in the seventeenth century there was adequate
provision for the poor, charges of witchcraft were apparently fewer. Here it
was normal for children to support their parents in old age and infirmity, so
there were fewer pauper widows. There was an outburst of persecution of
witches in the 1640s, a time of great economic hardship.

Belief in witchcraft could offer an alternative to Josselin's idea that God
directly intervenes in everyday life to punish us for our sins. It was simpler to
attribute personal disasters to the malevolent actions of a witch: once an old
lady had got a bad name, such accusations were the more likely to stick. Few
believed that they could protect themselves against the wrath of God, but
many believed that magic and charms could guard them against witches.
Witchcraft provided an explanation for otherwise inexplicable personal los-
ses and sufferings, for disease and the inefficacy of seventeenth-century
medicine.

A similar point might be made about belief in astrology. The stars could
be blamed rather than God's wrath: astrologers suggested ways of outwit-
ting the stars, as it was not possible to outwit God. Decline in belief in
astrology and witches among the educated came with increasing education
and an increasing conviction that the environment could be controlled.

6 The Bible

All truth was believed to be contained in the Bible, the inspired word of
God. If the Bible was not such a big book we should have considered making
it a set book for this course. *All* discussion of political and economic ideas in
the early seventeenth century was based on the Bible; all writing, from the
propaganda pamphlets of the civil war to the poems of Milton, Marvell and
Dryden, was drenched with Biblical idioms and allusions. Whether or not
you accept the validity of the Bible yourself, you must for the purposes of
this course acquaint yourselves with its main themes.

In the persons of our ancestors, Adam and Eve, mankind fell from
Paradise at the beginning of history. Since then all men and women are
naturally sinful. The life and death of Christ on earth overcame this sinful-
ness for those who believe. The Old Testament depicts the history of the
chosen people, the Jews; the New Testament extends the possibility of salvation to all nations. But many seventeenth-century Englishmen (including
John Milton) saw the English as in a special sense a chosen people, heirs to
the promises which God had made to the Jews. At the end of time Christ will

come to earth again to condemn the wicked to eternal torment, and his resurrected saints will live in bliss to all eternity.

The great Biblical legends – Cain who slew his younger brother Abel, Jacob who supplanted his elder brother Esau, Noah whose family survived in the ark when the whole world was submerged in the Flood, Moses who led the Jews from captivity in Egypt to the promised land of Israel, Judas who betrayed Christ with a kiss, Peter who denied Christ in the hour of trial, Saul the persecutor who was miraculously transformed into St Paul the Apostle, the Dragon, the Beast and the Whore of the Apocalypse, who were all believed to personify Antichrist, the great enemy of Christianity – these occur again and again in writings of the seventeenth century. They supplied the metaphors and formed the idiom in which men spoke and thought. You must get used to this.

For most Englishmen the Bible was a relatively new book, freely available only for two generations before 1618. Before the Reformation the Bible in the vernacular was forbidden. The clergy read it in Latin (if they were literate); special permission was required for laymen to read it in English. Heretics studied manuscript translations at the risk of their lives. With Henry VIII's Reformation an English printed Bible was authorized. But it was suppressed under Mary (1553–8), when some three hundred Englishmen, mostly from the middling and lower classes, were burnt for heresy (the Marian martyrs). Under Elizabeth (1558–1603) English versions of the Bible circulated again; under James I the translation which we know as the Authorized Version appeared in 1611. It was a great piece of good fortune that the Authorized Version was translated into superb prose. Try to read it rather than any later translation. Its influence as a model of style for most seventeenth-century writers was very great and almost always beneficial. The recent availability of the Bible in English was thus an exciting cultural event. There was a marked increase in literacy in England in the century after the Reformation, partly stimulated by desire to read the Bible. Increased lay literacy, in its turn, forced an improvement in the educational standards of the clergy in response to lay criticism. Because all truth was in the Bible, men searched it very carefully; any educated man or woman would recognize a Biblical allusion. By the 1640s, Thomas Hobbes thought many 'boys and wenches' had 'read the Scriptures once or twice over'.

The fact that an authorized version was necessary shows how important the Bible was. Some early translations had marginal notes glossing the text in what authority regarded as a seditious manner. Henry VIII had tried to prevent the lower classes from reading the Bible, and all classes from discussing it in public. That proved unenforceable once the printed Bible was available. So by the seventeenth century, with literacy descending the social scale, all sorts of simple people, with no historical sense at all, were scanning the Scriptures for solutions to the problems which beset their society. Take, for instance, a young Welshman, Rhys Evans, who came to London in 1629. Before he came to the City, he tells us, 'I looked upon the Scripture as a history of things that passed in other countries, pertaining to other persons; but now I looked upon it as a mystery to be opened at this time, pertaining also to us'.

Men hungry for the Word applied to the England of their day the prophecies with which the Bible abounds. Interpreting them became a major interest: we shall return to this in Block 6, 'Millenarianism'. Before 1640 books interpreting Biblical prophecies were liable to be suppressed by the censor; after 1640 the censorship collapsed, and they abounded. Censorship was restored in the early '50s only with difficulty.

EXERCISE

What would you expect to be the main implications and consequences of living in a society all of whose members were deemed to be Christians and where the Bible was believed to be the inspired Word of God?

DISCUSSION

Since men thought that God intervened in day-to-day life, it was important for them to know what his wishes and intentions were. God could communicate directly with individuals in response to prayer, but the main normal source of guidance was thought to be the Bible.

In particular, the Biblical prophecies, if properly understood, might hold the key to the perplexing events of these difficult decades. Rhys Evans came to believe that the prophet Amos and Revelation Chapters 8 and 11 gave an account of the English civil war. This is an extreme but not unparalleled case.

The Bible could also be used for negative-critical purposes. Since it contains all that we need to know, anything not in the Bible must be suspect. Many Puritans could not find bishops there; Milton could not find the Trinity; a Leveller could find no reference to 40-shilling freeholders (who composed the Parliamentary electorate in English counties); he concluded, not very logically, that therefore the Bible favoured manhood suffrage.

As this example suggests, men found what they wanted in the Bible: many of course found justifications for the hierarchical society in which they lived, such as the subordination of women. But the point is that they looked there, and their arguments seemed more convincing if they had Biblical backing, their allusions more forceful when conveyed through a Biblical metaphor. When Milton wanted to express his utter disgust with the return of monarchy in 1660, he said that the English people had chosen themselves 'a captain back for Egypt' – the land of slavery from which Moses had delivered the Israelites.

EXERCISE

In the light of what I have been saying about metaphorical uses of the Bible, read carefully the following passage from Gerrard Winstanley the Digger, and try to express its meaning in modern political terms. It was published in April 1649, three months after the execution of Charles I as a traitor to the people of England, three weeks after the Diggers had set up their first communist colony.

> Esau, the man of flesh, which is covetousness and pride, hath killed Jacob, the spirit of meekness and righteous government in the light of reason, and rules over him. And so the earth, that was made a common treasury for all to live comfortably upon, is become through man's unrighteous actions one over another, to be a place wherein one torments another . . . The earth hath been enclosed and given to the elder brother Esau, or man of flesh, and hath been bought and sold from one to another; and Jacob, or the younger brother, is made a servant . . .
>
> Therefore you powers of the earth, or Lord Esau the elder brother, because you have appeared to rule the creation, first take notice that . . . Jacob . . . is the seed that lies hid in and among the poor common people, or younger brother, out of whom the blessing of deliverance is to rise and spring up to all nations. . . . The time is now come for thy downfall. . . . Jacob hath been very low, but he is rising and will rise, do the worst thou canst; and the poor people whom thou oppresses shall be the saviours of the land.

DISCUSSION

Esau, who abused the position of elder brother, represents the ruling class; Jacob represents 'the poor common people' from whom salvation shall come. But salvation is not something other-worldly for Winstanley; it means the establishment of a communist society on earth, now. The passage is a call to action at a time when, as Winstanley put it, 'the present state of the old world . . . is running up like parchment in the fire', and anything seemed possible. The vocabulary is Biblical, but the message is political.

Here is another example from Thomas Hobbes, the political thinker whose *Leviathan* you will be studying later in the course. He writes 'Of the maintenance of our Saviour and his Apostles, we read only that they had a purse (which was carried by Judas Iscariot)'.

EXERCISE

Recalling the discussion of tithes, what do you think Hobbes is saying?

DISCUSSION

You have got the point, I hope? The clergy, maintained by tithe payments, are compared to Judas, the betrayer of Christ. Hobbes's point is as clear as it is witty. But nobody could deny the factual accuracy of what he says. It is only by implication abusive. Many others as well as Hobbes used Biblical phraseology *because* they wanted to convey unorthodox messages. It was safer. Hobbes, you will remember, thought the bishops would like to burn him. Such passages as the above suggest he may have been right.

Thus even men whose interests were not primarily theological continually echoed the Bible. We shall be looking later at Francis Bacon, Andrew Marvell and Sir Isaac Newton, as well as at Hobbes and Winstanley. You must get the feel of this Biblicism if you are to appreciate the literature and propaganda of the period. We shall be observing in this course the gradual emergence of 'rational', 'scientific' explanations to replace simpler explanations in terms of the will of God. The first men to put forward serious philosophical arguments which did *not* derive from the Bible shocked their contemporaries.

Of course people read the Bible differently, and found different things in it. Biblical literalists tended to be those who thought the Reformation had not gone far enough in England, who wanted to get rid of 'remnants of popery' and return to the purity of the primitive church. These we call Puritans if they stayed within the Church of England, sectaries or separatists if they left it, whether for exile or for an illegal underground existence at home.

EXERCISE

I have used the word 'Puritan'. Before we discuss it any further, jot down what the word means for you.

DISCUSSION

It is a word that is used in many ways. One modern sense of the word is 'killjoy', and this sense is often applied to seventeenth-century Puritans. They are thought of as gloomy men wearing black clothes, whining psalms through their noses, going about desecrating churches, shutting theatres and trying in general to stop people enjoying themselves.

There were people like that in seventeenth-century England, but we must not start by assuming that those whom we call 'Puritans' in the seventeenth century were 'puritanical' in the sense that some nineteenth-century nonconformists were. Main-line Puritans were certainly not killjoys. Oliver Cromwell loved music and wine; Milton loved music and the theatre; Bunyan's fiddle and flute can still be seen in Bedford; his Pilgrims dance, drink wine and spirits.

For our present purpose we should emphasize that Puritans attached more importance to preaching and discussion than to the sacramental aspects of religion which Catholics stressed. Those whom we come to call 'Laudians' inside the Church of England (after Archbishop Laud), shared the Catholic view that the ceremonies and sacraments of the church were as important as 'preaching the word'.

In this period I personally prefer to contrast 'Puritans' with 'Laudians' rather than with 'Anglicans' as some do. 'Anglican' means member of the national church, the church to which all Englishmen and women belonged. To contrast Puritans with Anglicans is like saying that the two main parties in English politics today are Englishmen and socialists. Francis Bacon indeed said that those whom their enemies called 'Puritans' were 'the greatest body of the subjects'. Only from 1662 were former 'Puritans' excluded from the state church; after that it is accurate to contrast Anglicans and nonconformists, although many of the latter regarded themselves as the true heirs of the Elizabethan and Jacobean church. I have tried to be consistent in my use of the word 'Puritan' but you will find it used in other ways by some of the writers whom you will read on this course. The important thing is to be aware that it is a slippery word, and to be on the look out.

Puritanism tended to be an individualistic creed, and Puritans tended to be critical of authority (see *C of R*, pp 89–90). The Laudians thought men should be wary of individual interpretations of the Bible which conflicted with the traditions of the church; reliance on the light within each man's conscience, they argued, must lead to anarchy. As we shall see, they had a point.

7 Rival cultures?

Analogous to the wish to return to the purity of the primitive church was the wish to get back to the freedom which (some said) Englishmen had enjoyed before the Norman Conquest. Men were a little hazy about what life had been like in the days of the free Anglo-Saxons; but many agreed that the 'Norman Yoke' had subverted the laws and liberties of Englishmen, that English history since 1066 had been a struggle to recover Anglo-Saxon freedom, with Magna Carta one of the milestones on the way. This theory appealed especially to lawyers like Sir Edward Coke and to those MPs who suspected that the Stuart kings had absolutist aspirations. The 'backward look' forms one of the many links between common lawyers and Puritans.

We must be careful not to over-simplify here. As the seventeenth-century crisis developed (see Kevin Wilson's discussion, p 53 et seq) so different sorts of intellectual attitudes divided Englishmen in different ways. In *C of R* I discussed this under headings such as 'Court and Country', 'Conflict in the Arts', and more generally in Chapter 6. Look again at these pages in the light of what I have been saying here, and compare them with P. W. Thomas in the Reader, article 21. (We shall return to these problems in Block 2, *A Changing Culture*.)

So we can see contrasts between the Puritan appeal to the Bible and the Laudian emphasis on the ceremonies and sacraments of the church; between the constitutionalism of the common lawyers and Strafford's and Laud's emphasis on efficiency; between traditional relations of dependence and communal solidarity and the cash nexus which was spreading through society. Individualism seemed to be subverting traditional standards of community, of hierarchy, of degree. Some – especially academics in the universities – thought all secular wisdom had been discovered by the classics of Greece and Rome: others more optimistically believed with Francis Bacon that the Moderns had improved on the Ancients and could do so still more. Puritans could set the authority of the Bible against the authority of the classics, and so it was paradoxically easier for them to support the Moderns. (We return to this subject in Block 3, *A Divided Society*.) In art, Italianate styles tended to be favoured in court circles; the more homely and realistic Dutch art appealed to simpler men who did not fail to note that the Dutch were protestants, Italianate artists favoured by the court mostly Catholics. As you will see in Television programme 1, the greater gentry built their houses of stone – a status symbol because it was more expensive; merchants and lesser gentry were beginning to build in brick. Often the bricks were imported from the Netherlands (where they were cheap), and with them came Dutch styles in architecture. The contrast between the florid and the plain style extended even to sermons (see *C of R* pp 156–7, and *The Development of Prose*).

A whole series of alternatives thus opened up in the changing culture. It is of course by no means the case that a Puritan in the church would necessarily be a Parliamentarian in politics and a defender of the Moderns. When men lined up for civil war in 1642 there were Puritan gentlemen and royalist yeomen; and we should certainly not think of England as divided or even dividing into two camps before 1642. But the elements of two different cultures were forming. It is of the essence of metaphysical poetry, Arnold Kettle argues in 'Metaphysical Poetry' Block 2, that it accepts and attempts to overcome contradictions.

Even more difficult to assess is what some have seen as a third culture of radical elements among the lower classes. In religion this involved putting the spirit above the letter of the Bible, a reliance on what Quakers were to call 'the inner light'. In politics it meant rejecting much existing law altogether, as something whose object was merely to protect the property of the rich; in economics it tended to produce communist theories. More traditional and less radical was lower-class acceptance of the semi-magical remedies of alchemists and folk doctors. The morris dances and popular festivals which Puritans wanted to suppress were another expression of traditional lower-class culture; for a short time the popular tradition of the great age of Elizabethan and Jacobean drama was closely linked with this culture.

But I am anticipating points which will be taken up later. Before 1640 it was not always easy for Puritans to express their views, because of the censorship; and the last three volumes of Sir Edward Coke's great but partisan summary of English law, the *Institutes*, could not be published before 1640. Sectaries and the forerunners of those whom we later call Levellers and Diggers were even less able to make their views known. It is not even certain that lower-class opposition took any more theoretical form than resentment of the gentry, and of middlemen and speculators who undermined traditional ideas of how society should operate. But it was shown in sporadic group resistance to enclosure, in riots against high prices, riots in defence of traditional rights of commoners in forests and fens.

At this stage all I want to suggest is that, among the alternative choices facing society which we shall be following in this course, we should not forget the people of England who 'have not spoken yet'. After 1640 they had the opportunity to speak, and their ideas swiftly gained coherence and system. When I use the word 'radical' in this course I intend it to apply to representatives or spokesmen of this third culture – to separatist sectaries in religion, to political reformers dissatisfied with the rule of the gentry and merchants whom Parliament represented (Levellers, Diggers, Fifth Monarchists), to scientific and educational reformers who rejected the dominant establishment of the College of Physicians, Oxford and Cambridge universities.

Some historians would think it exaggerated to talk of two (or three) rival cultures in the seventeenth century; and they would rightly insist that even if we can isolate such cultures for analysis there were no hard and fast lines dividing them. I want only to give you a possible hypothesis, which you must test for yourself as the course proceeds. By the end I hope you will have your own ideas. I should be surprised – and a little disappointed – if they coincided entirely with mine!

A Changing Economy

So far we have been looking at seventeenth-century England in a static way, comparing then with now. But English society was far from static in the seventeenth century, and our title suggests that a main object of this course is to look at *changes* in English culture.

EXERCISE

Please read Lawrence Stone in your Reader (article 1). What does this extract tell us about the changing nature of English economic and social structure at this time?

DISCUSSION

Stone's article is a brilliant but very condensed survey of a mass of material which it is difficult to digest all at once. I hope you will return to it as the course progresses and see how Stone's arguments fit in with what you have learnt. At the moment you have to take it on trust.

Important points to stress for our present purposes are I think:

1 The changes concerned affected all Europe; but they were especially acute in England – 'a seismic upheaval of unprecedented magnitude' are strong words for a scholar to use. Why was England different?

2 The population explosion was slowing down after 1620, the very beginning of our period. Some historians would extend the period of rapid population growth for another decade or more, into the 1630s; and in any case the consequences of the population explosion would take a long time to work out: men born in the 1620s would come to maturity in the '40s and '50s.

3 The price revolution covers roughly the same period; prices are rising less sharply after 1640. (Glance at the tables in Appendix C of *C of R* which illustrate this point.)

4 In consequence of the population explosion and the price revolution the century before 1640 was 'the century of mobility'.

5 This age of great social mobility was also the great age of Puritanism. Were the two connected, and if so how?

There is a great deal here to think about (and test) as the course proceeds. At the moment you should treat the last point only as a hypothesis. But points 1–4 are relatively non-controversial. One or two aspects of Stone's analysis are worth considering a little more:

(a) Stone's 'hierarchy of status . . . corresponded roughly' with the 'hierarchy of incomes'. But social mobility among his groups 4 to 6 means that as some men grow richer so they can be absorbed socially into a higher group. (You will meet an example of this in Television programme 1: Stephen Proctor, the industrialist who bought Fountains.) Already some merchants are in Tawney's expressive phrase 'as rich as peers'. The status hierarchy is far from being fixed, as those at the top were learning to their discomfiture.

(b) Groups 1 to 3 in Stone's 'status hierarchy' comprise 90–95 per cent of the population, and among them there is either no social mobility or downward mobility. That means that the vast majority of the English people have no share in the expansive economic activities which lead to the enrichment of the fortunate few. The irresistible consequence of rising prices is that most of the poor get poorer. Food prices rise faster than other prices, and much faster than wages. The price of barley, which makes the bread and beer which are the staples of the diet of the poor, rises faster than the price of wheat, the bread of the well-to-do.

(c) But – and this I am sure is a point Lawrence Stone would have stressed more if he had been writing today – some members of his group 3 manage to escape from the poverty trap. *Some* yeomen, artisans and traders who were very lucky and lived near an expanding market (the London food market, for instance – see (e) below) could profit sufficiently to be able to accumulate money with which they could buy out their less fortunate fellow villagers, for whom 'downward mobility' meant that they had to sell land, as John Bunyan's ancestors had done in Bedfordshire, leaving him to earn his living as a tinker. (You will be reading about Bunyan later, in Block 9.)

Social historians have recently drawn special attention to this minority of Stone's group 3 (which might be called 3A) as contrasted with the majority for whom there was no escape from permanent poverty: let us call the latter 3B. In the seventeenth century 'village élites' from group 3A are establishing themselves as subordinate rulers of parishes under the gentry. From them village constables and churchwardens are drawn; they comprise parish vestries. They co-operate with JPs in implementing the poor law, codified in the starvation years at the end of Elizabeth's reign, which copes with group 3B and keeps it in its place. They help JPs to control ale-houses, the social centres of the poor. They present 'sinners' to church courts for judgement. These village élites tend to have little sympathy with traditional village customs and rituals which interfere with labour discipline, such as the traditional Sunday sports encouraged by James I and Charles I. (We shall be looking at their loss of sympathy for the régime in Block 3, *A Divided Society*.) Puritan 'sabbatarianism' appeals to them on law-and-order grounds, as well as (perhaps) on religious grounds. The growing Puritan conviction that the mass of the poor were inherently wicked would also fit their way of thinking (see Wrightson and Levine, *Poverty and Piety in an English Village*, and Hunt, *The Puritan Moment, passim*). We can understand Keith Thomas's point that before and during our period conflicts between the groups we have called 3A and 3B 'grew particularly acute' (Reader, article 3). By the end of our period, Stone rightly observes, 'the topmost elements of group 3' (our group 3A) were merging with 'the lowest elements of group 4' and 'beginning to form another status group of their own'.

(d)   Stone's points 1 to 4 above help to account for the political revolution of the 1640s: see pp 66–8 below. The slowing down of population expansion and the price rise may have contributed to the re-stabilization which occurred after 1660. My points (a) and (c) above may help to explain how by the end of our period 'the potentialities for social and political control' had 'greatly increased', since whereas in 1522 only about one village in ten had a resident squire, by 1680 the proportion had shot up to over two-thirds. Compare what Joan Thirsk has to say in the Reader (article 7) about the greater docility of villages living under the eye of a resident squire, and then ask yourself: 'Where had this vast increase in the number of gentlemen come from?' They must be men who had climbed up the 'hierarchy of incomes' to a new position in the 'hierarchy of status'.

What ideas had they brought with them? They were unlikely to accept the traditional modes of thought of those they replaced, just as those whom they joined almost certainly modified their attitudes in the process of making enough money to maintain their high social position. During the revolutionary period Thomas Hobbes stressed that change stimulated mental activity, 'it being almost all one for a man to be always sensible of the same thing and not to be sensible of anything'. Again, these are points to which we shall return later in the course: keep your eye on them.

(e)   Stone was not concerned with the relation of the population explosion to the food supply, but it is a question which we must raise. Between 1500 and 1660 the population more than doubled. The supply of food cannot have increased at anything like that rate. In the same period the proportion of men and women living in towns increased; so did the proportion dependent on wage labour. These people no longer grew their own food. There can be no doubt that the majority of the population ate less well at the beginning of our period than their grandfathers and great-grandfathers had done. Even so, the England of 1618 had to import corn. By 1689 England was a corn-exporting country, even though the urban and wage-earning sector of the community must have grown still further. A series of agricultural changes made possible this spectacular economic reversal – new crops, new techniques, bringing new land under cultivation – as well as significant changes in the law and the attitudes of governments. We shall be looking at this in Block 4, *The Revolution and Its Impact*. Here we should emphasize that growing more food might increase social tensions – between fen-drainers, or gentlemen enclosing wastes or forests, and those poorer people whose livelihood depended on such land remaining communal property.

(f) If you look at Joan Thirsk in your Reader (article 7) you will see that new industries were developing in the early seventeenth century. A new, non-agricultural, non-traditional society was expanding both in towns and in some areas of the countryside. The power of money was increasing; so was the new importance of education as opposed to birth. All this tended to call in question the traditional caste system and its values. But this system and these values had great staying power. Most men and women were illiterate, took their ideas from their parson and their social superiors. It needed the revolution of the '40s and '50s to produce theories of political and social democracy, demands for universal education, and for a society in which careers were open to the talented. One of the aims of this course is to help you to decide how far new views triumphed in practice over the old during this revolution, how far a new social structure was created.

An Individual in a Changing Society

I have referred many times already to Ralph Josselin. The time has come to get to know him better. His life – 1618–83 – almost exactly spans the period of our course. He was born into the household of a yeoman who was, through unsuccessful farming and unwise land purchases, depleting his inheritance – downward mobility! Josselin early decided that he wanted to become a clergyman, and finally persuaded his father to send him to Cambridge. His parents were too poor to support him at the university, and he had to interrupt his studies at frequent intervals to take temporary jobs. After getting his degree he began to look for a living. First he was a schoolmaster in Bedfordshire for a couple of years, then a curate in Buckinghamshire at £14 a year plus meals. In September 1640 he moved to an Essex living worth £44 a year, on which he could afford to get married – especially as he was teaching as well. In 1641 he got a better offer from Earls Colne in Essex, of £80 a year. He moved there in March 1641 and remained as its vicar until his death. In 1660 he conformed to the restored church, Puritan though he was; but he avoided using the prayer book for three years, and only started wearing the surplice three years before he died.

At Earls Colne, as his Diary reveals, Josselin was economically dependent on the local gentry, to whom he showed humble deference. On 15 January 1650 'Mr Wade of Halsted sent me a dozen of candle, and Mr Hickford a sugar-loaf, a liberal and bounteous gift; its an act of Thy love and goodness towards me and I desire to give Thee oh Lord the praise of Thy mercy. Mrs Church gave me 5 shillings, but none in the town [i.e. village] sent me any considerable gift else but old Spooner' (*Diary*, p 188).

Josselin received from Parliament an addition of £40 to his stipend, but it was paid irregularly. However, despite continual complaints of the failure of his parishioners to pay him his dues, Josselin prospered. In addition to his clerical activities, he farmed – much more successfully than his father. His estate rose steadily in value to £100 in 1650, over £400 in 1654, £900 by 1658. His biographer estimates that he might be worth £2,000 by the time of his death, even though he had given his daughter a dowry of £200 (Macfarlane, *The Family Life of Ralph Josselin*, p 58). So in his capacity as farmer he is a member of the prospering group 3A.

I have already referred to his Diary to illustrate the prevalence of disease, pain and infant mortality in the seventeenth century ('A Different World', pp 6, 10). Josselin was something of a hypochondriac, but his own and his family's health gave him plenty to worry about. He regularly records information about the weather; the harvest is vital not only to himself as a farmer but also to the well-being of his parishioners and to the tithe payments he hopes to receive from them. I noted Josselin's sorrow at his children's deaths, and he served as an example of the economic uncertainties of life in an age before insurance. Both individual and national disasters, Josselin thought, were punishments for our sins ('A Different World', p 16). In February 1649 he worried lest the nation should be held responsible to God for the execution of Charles I. When he heard the news of the final defeat of the radical Levellers at Burford in May 1649, he recorded it as 'a glorious rich providence of God to England' (*Diary*, p 167). (The significance of the Leveller threat will be made clear in Block 5, *Political Ideas*.)

EXERCISE

Please read through the extracts from Josselin's Diary printed in the Anthology (extract 61), and see what other information about the society you can squeeze or tease out of them.

DISCUSSION

Obviously there is no 'correct' answer to this question. I wouldn't be surprised if you found many things that I missed. Here are mine:

1   Josselin illustrates the precariousness of life for small farmers in group 3A near the margin between prosperity and poverty. 'The times are very sad and full of difficulties' he wrote in February 1649, when he was concerned about responsibility for executing the King; 'and yet God provideth for me and mine.' It was passages of this sort that led me to speculate about possible links between economic insecurity and Calvinist doctrines of predestination ('A Different World', p 13).

2   In the '40s and '50s Josselin was very aware of the disturbing presence of the sometimes irregularly paid Army. 'Through mercy' he escaped in September 1647 from having 'somewhat bold and vapouring' troops billeted on him. (The summer of 1647 saw the peak of revolutionary ferment in the Army; we take this up in Block 5, *Political Ideas*.) Four months earlier he had 'some rugged words from . . . a Lieutenant about quartering', which made him reflect 'how unable poor men are to contain their spirits, if ever they are in employment'. In a normal army – as opposed to the Parliament's New Model – poor men would not be made lieutenants; the behaviour of this one confirmed Josselin's traditional Puritan view that it was risky to give the poor the chance of getting above themselves.

3   Josselin is permanently worried about his income, about the failure of parishioners to pay him his dues, and of the threat, as he sees it, that tithe payments may be abolished (20 September 1647). By June 1650 some men wondered whether 'any standing ministry in England' would continue, and Josselin's anxiety extended till July. The danger, as he saw it, came especially from Anabaptists and Quakers (July 1653, July 1655).

4   Josselin's activities in many ways fit rather neatly into the picture of a fusion of interests between Puritans and parish élites. In May 1647 he encouraged the parish officers to punish 'the rudeness of divers about the congregation'. The poor, he noted in September, are especially 'careless of the Sabbath' and profane. Men were reluctant to turn out to church on a wet day (30 August 1648); compulsion was lacking since the breakdown of the old church courts. (cf. 'A Changing Economy', p 24).

5   Josselin's political anxieties in the 1650s drove him to a serious study of Thomas Brightman and other millenarian writers whose books speculating that the end of the world was at hand proliferated once the Laudian censorship had broken down in 1640. 'The Lord maketh me still inquisitive after the times and seasons': are they leading 'to the coming of Christ'? His millenarian interests seem to have lapsed in the relatively quiet mid-'50s but they returned after 1660. But he was still capable of political shrewdness, as in his comment of 25 January 1660: 'the nation looking more to Charles Stuart out of love to themselves, not him'.

6   The reference to 'my reconciler' on 2 February 1649 is to a collection of apparently contradictory Biblical texts which Josselin began assembling and reconciling. Obviously this was in order to combat those radical sectaries who were calling the authority of the Bible in question. The interest did not survive the suppression of such critics after the Blasphemy Ordinance of 1650.

These points can be further illustrated from parts of the Diary not reproduced in the Anthology. It is relevant to Josselin's financial worries (3 above) that in mid-September 1647 he complained that people were 'careless of the worship of God' and paid their tithes unwillingly (*Diary*, p 136). Nine years later he quotes one of his own parishioners, reluctantly agreeing to pay a churchwarden's rate, as saying that 'he had rather give money to pull the church down and lay it in the highway' (*Diary*, p 366). Many passages illustrate (4) by showing Josselin in the rather agreeable role of mediator between his parishioners, making up differences to prevent law-suits. It must have given him great pleasure when in November 1644 he 'read an order whereby alehouses are in the power of the well-affected and the minister of the parish' (*Diary*, p 27). His millenarian obsession (5) extends to a dream of England carrying the kingdom of Christ by force of arms to France. In 1653 Josselin records his conviction that 'the last days draw near', though he was not convinced, as many were, that 1656 was the year (*Diary*, pp 219–28, 307). A further point, which Josselin's editor makes, is that there is not a single direct reference to hell or damnation in all the 660 large pages of the Diary (Macfarlane, *The Family Life of Ralph Josselin*, p 168). Since it is clear that Josselin is in some unmistakable sense a Puritan, this is worth reflecting on. Puritanism and Puritans were perhaps more concerned with this world than with the next.

Finally we may ask how far we can generalize from Josselin; how typical was he of Englishmen of his time? He was a parson, and a Puritan. Parsons formed less than 0.5 per cent of the population; Puritans a much larger but unascertainable proportion. Josselin was also a yeoman farmer in his own right, relatively well-to-do. He was above the 90–95 per cent of the population who form Stone's groups 1–3. His Diary tells us only at second hand what life was like for the vast majority of the population. This should warn us against generalizing from a single source, or from the experience of one man, a member of a particular profession and a particular social and economic class.

The mere fact that Josselin kept a diary makes him different. Why did he keep it? What sort of facts did he choose to put in, and what do you suppose he leaves out? The seventeenth century is a great period for diaries. Pepys and Evelyn are two of the best-known diarists, but there are many more. Kevin Wilson quotes (in 'England and Europe') Sir William Brereton, Sydenham Poyntz and John Rous. And diaries are only one example of many similar kinds of writing – biographies and autobiographies, for instance, accounts of religious conversion and spiritual autobiographies like Bunyan's *Grace Abounding*. What is the explanation of this fashion?

It has something to do, I think (as I suggested in *C of R,* pp 217–18) with a growing individualism, an increasing self-consciousness, as well as with an extension of literacy. The protestant emphasis on the individual conscience (rather than the institution of the church) as crucial to salvation led to soul-searching, to probing one's own motives, testing one's own sincerity – as Josselin does. Very many diaries started as a form of the 'spiritual book-keeping' recommended by Puritan preachers. Even Samuel Pepys, whose diary records his amorous exploits and his acceptance of bribes, continually tries to assess his spiritual as well as his financial balance sheet.

The age emphasized introspection and the identification of individual characteristics – whether in the portraits discussed in Radio programme 3, in the 'character' which was a specific literary form, or in the great individualists of Elizabethan and Jacobean drama from Marlowe's Faustus and Tamberlaine to Shakespeare's Hamlet and Richard II. When you come to look at metaphysical poetry in Block 2 you will find Arnold Kettle distinguishing it as *private* as opposed to *public* poetry.

Printing made possible private reading for many of the middling sort; the more comfortable households in which they lived, the greater domestic privacy which rising prosperity brought, not to mention glass windows and spectacles, made reading a less hazardous occupation. Protestants, of course, read mainly the Bible; they interpreted it according to their individual consciences. You will soon be reading Bunyan's *The Pilgrim's Progress,* which starts with the hero running away to save his own soul, stopping his ears to keep out the cries of his wife and family. The great classics of Puritan literature – not only *Pilgrim's Progress* but also *Paradise Lost, Paradise Regained, Samson Agonistes, Robinson Crusoe* and *Clarissa Harlowe* – portray an *individual* working out his or her salvation *alone.* At the beginning of our period all Englishmen were born into the national church; at the end they choose which voluntary congregation they wish to worship in. It is the same with

Figure 1   Portrait believed to be Ralph Josselin. (Reproduced from a photograph supplied by Essex County Record Office by permission of Mrs S. Sherwood.)

Figure 2   Entries for 13 January 1650 from the manuscript of Josselin's Diary. (Photograph by Dr Alan Macfarlane, reproduced by permission of Colonel R. H. C. Probert.)

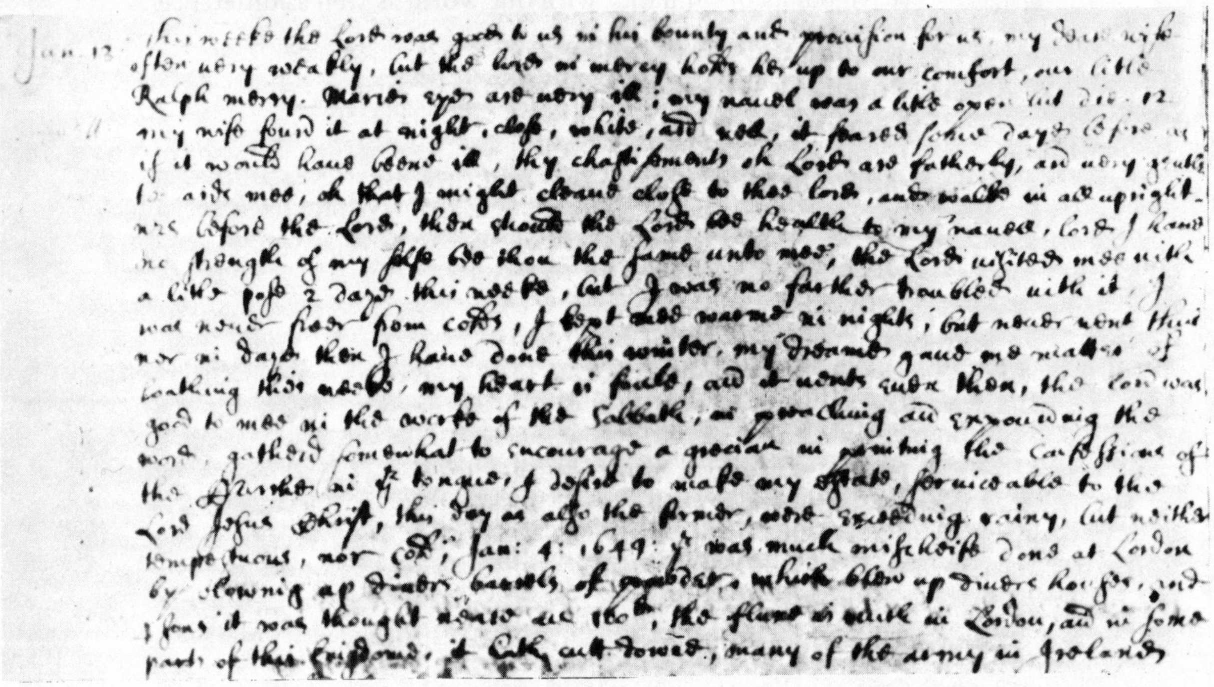

Jan: 13. This weeke the Lord was good to us in his bounty and provision for us, my deare wife often very weakly, but the lord in mercy holds her up to our comfort, our litle Ralph merry. Maries eyes are very ill; my navel was a litle open but die 12 [on the twelfth] my wife found it at night, close, white, and well, it feared some dayes before as if it would have beene ill, thy chastisements oh Lord are fatherly, and very gentle towards mee, oh that I might cleave close to thee lord, and walke in all uprightnes before the Lord, then should the Lord bee health to my navell, lord I have no strength of myselfe bee thou the same unto mee, the Lord visited mee with a litle pose [cold] 2 dayes this weeke, but I was no farther troubled with it, I was never freer from colds, I kept mee warme in nights, but never went thinner in dayes then I have done this winter, my dreames gave me matter of loathing this weeke, my heart is foule, and it vents even then, the lord was good to mee in the worke of the Sabbath, in preaching and expounding the word, gatherd somewhat to encourage a grecian in printing the Confessions of the Churches in their tongue, I desire to make my estate serviceable to the Lord Jesus Christ, this day as also the former, were exceeding rainy, but neither tempestuous, nor cold; Jan: 4: 1649: there was much mischiefe done at London by blowing up divers barrels of powder, which blew up divers houses, and persons it was thought neare an 100 d., the fluxe is much in London, and in some parts of this kingdome, it hath cutt downe many of the army in Ireland political thought. The greatest English political theorist of the century, Thomas Hobbes, starts from men as isolated individuals. So in their different ways do the Levellers and Milton. Many of the Parliamentarians stressed the rights and liberties of individuals, including the right to property, as the foundation of politics. John Locke made a theory of it. (This anticipates points which will be discussed in Blocks 5, 7 and 10.)

Keith Thomas attributed persecution of witches to a conflict between a growing individualism, an ethic of self-help, and the traditional ethos of the village community ('A Different World', p 17). The village élites whom we discussed above had become élites because of their individualistic disregard for the older communal ethos; they used their ruling position to impose new standards. Solving the problem of feeding England's increased population likewise involved a ruthless individualism and disregard for traditional communal rights (Reader, Stone, article 1). The seventeenth century saw this conflict worked out at all levels – individual conscience versus national church, self-interest versus communal solidarity, the right to do what one would with one's property as against one's responsibility for one's neighbour, and so on. Individualism won out so completely in the seventeenth century and later that by the present century remedial action by the state was needed to protect weaker and less fortunate members of society (the welfare state). So here perhaps controversies going on in the seventeenth century have points of similarity with our world as well as difference.

England and Europe

1 Introduction

Aim

The aim of this section is to consider the place of England in Europe during the period covered by our course – though greater emphasis is given to developments in the first half of the seventeenth century. This section will not attempt to cover the history of Europe in this period, nor will it provide a systematic treatment of English foreign policy. It will attempt to show how seventeenth-century English people (and institutions) responded to European issues and how present-day historians have taken different views about the nature of seventeenth-century European developments.

I've approached the subject with the following considerations in mind:

1 Foreign policy issues played a part in the constitutional crisis in England.

2 The phenomenon of 'crisis' is not something which can be uniquely applied to England in this period.

3 Political, social and cultural developments in seventeenth-century England can be illuminated by continental comparisons.

The section is organized in five sub-sections:

1 *English attitudes to Europe* This takes a fairly speculative view of different attitudes to, and perceptions of, Europe held by English people in the early seventeenth century.

2 *English policy towards Europe 1618–40* This considers England's relationships with the major European powers. It also deals with the way that foreign affairs impinged directly on English politics and helped to widen the gulf between the government and its critics.

3 *Court and country* This considers the significance of the Court versus Country antithesis in explaining the breakdown in the English political consensus but gives the issue a wider context by raising questions about the relationship of the seventeenth-century state to European society.

4 *The general crisis of the seventeenth century* This introduces the vexed problem of 'crisis in Europe', presents several fundamentally different interpretations of the question and considers the significance of this concept in understanding the processes at work in seventeenth-century England and Europe.

5 *Crisis in England: French and Dutch models of society* This final sub-section considers two different seventeenth-century potentialities:
(a) Was England to follow the European trend towards absolute monarchy exemplified by France?
(b) Was England to extend the power and effectiveness of representative institutions of government along Dutch lines?

2 English attitudes to Europe

Figure 3 shows a map of Europe which gives an outline of the frontiers of the European states as they were just before the outbreak of the Thirty Years' War. Even a quick glance reveals major differences between then and now. These differences include:

1 the size of the large Kingdom of Poland in Eastern Europe;

2 the territorial presence of the Turkish Empire west of Constantinople;

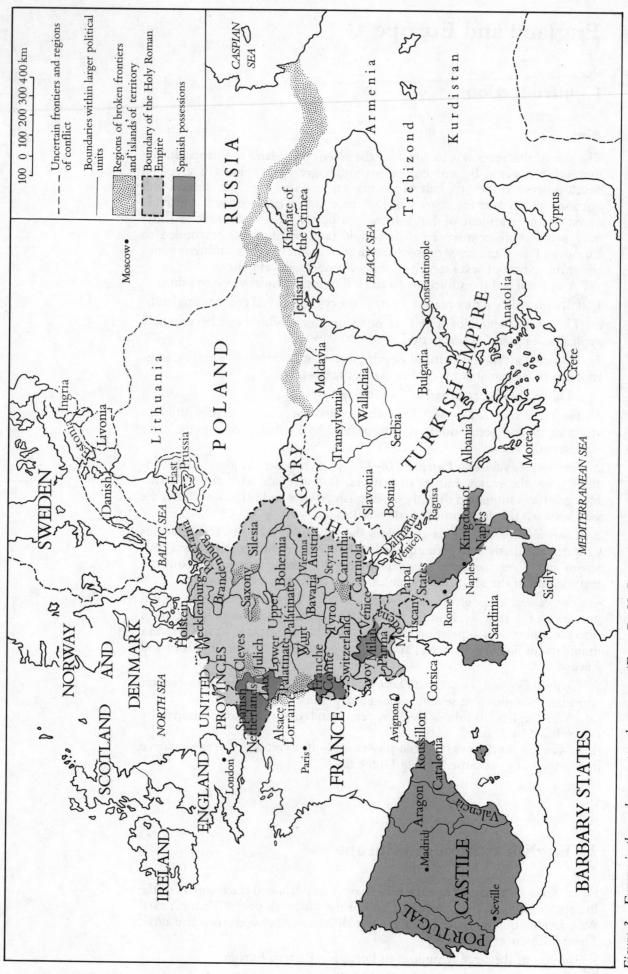

Figure 3   Europe in the early seventeenth century. (From D. H. Pennington (1970) A General History of Europe – Seventeenth Century Europe, Longman. Based on maps from P. Chauna La Civilisation de l'Europe Classique.)

3   the numerous states in central Europe, loosely termed the Holy Roman Empire;

4   the various states in the Italian peninsula;

5   the several Spanish dependencies far from the Iberian peninsula itself.

As the map shows, inter-state boundaries, particularly in eastern Europe, were much more fluid than the frontiers of today, but the map also illustrates that on *territorial* considerations alone, we are dealing with a different kind of Europe from the one we know today. We could extend this by introducing comparative data for such indices as size and density of population, patterns of land ownership, industrial and agricultural output, types of political system and so on. But rather than labour the comparison, I would like to look more closely at the way that seventeenth-century Europe looked – especially to English eyes.

Look at *Figure 4,* a reproduction of a map of Europe drawn in 1623. Maps like this could have been seen by contemporaries at, say, the premises of a London bookseller, or at the house of a wealthy merchant or in the library of the House of Commons. What did a seventeenth-century English person 'see' when he looked at a map like this? What meaning did Amsterdam, Paris, Madrid, Vienna and Rome have for seventeenth-century English eyes? Let us consider these issues in the following exercises.

EXERCISE

Please read the extracts from the Commons Debates of 1621 printed in the Anthology (extract 11). (1) What do these extracts tell us about parliamentary attitudes towards the English interest in European affairs? (2) What images do these MPs have of Europe?

DISCUSSION

I've noted down the following points:

1 (a)   support for the Palatinate as a symbol of the Protestant cause in Europe. See the Reader, Jones, article 4, for further elaboration;

(b)   opposition to Spain, traditional enemy, commercial rival in the New World and the leading Catholic power in Europe;

(c)   sympathy for the United Provinces in the Low Countries – 'they cannot subsist without us no more than our well-being without them';

(d)   distrust of the Roman Catholics in England – the enemy within.

In his opening address to the 1621 Parliament, James had requested a subsidy for the continued defence of the Palatinate without compromising his policy of alliance with Spain. These extracts show considerable parliamentary scepticism about the wisdom of such a policy. Members of Parliament were concerned not just with the question of the Palatinate but the wider cause of Protestantism in Europe – a cause it was claimed that was being undermined by James's policy towards Spain and the Habsburg Empire. In the event, Parliament was prepared to grant an immediate subsidy for the defence of the Palatinate and further supply following a general declaration of war in defence of the Protestant interest in Europe. This offer was coupled with a petition to the King that his son Charles should marry a Protestant princess. James replied that such an interference in 'deep matters of state' was an infringement of the prerogative and brought the debate to an end.

The conduct of foreign policy was essentially a matter of royal prerogative but such was the precarious nature of royal finances that the King could not support an army overseas for any length of time without obtaining additional revenue from Parliament. It would be too much of an exaggeration to see the 1621 debate on foreign policy as a challenge to the royal prerogative. But the debate shows that it was quite impossible to consider the granting of a subsidy without also discussing the uses to which a subsidy should be put. At least Parliament was not prepared to give the King a blank

AMERICÆ
PARS
Eſtotiland
Laborato-
ris terra
DROGEO

FRETUM DAVIS

GROENLANDIÆ PARS

Serelingers

M A

HYPERBOREUS

OCEANUS

Circulus Arcticus

D E U C A L E D O N I U S

O C E A N U S

Farre inſulæ

Hitland al: Scherland

OCCIDENS

50

40

HIBERNIA

SCOT

OCEANUS

GERMANI

CUS

ATLANTI

CANTA

BRICUS OCEA

NUS

CUS OCE

ANUS

H I S P A N I A

Mare Gallicum

Balearides inſ.

Mare Ibericum

MARE

Tyrrhenum et

Inferum

Canariæ I.

BARBA

RIA

AFRICÆ PARS

Miliaria Germanica. Duyſche Mylen.

10 20 30 40 50 60 70 80 90 100 110 120

20

30

40

cheque. In the words of Sir Richard Grosvenor it is 'not seasonable to give till it please the King to let us know our enemy'.

2 In considering the question of the images Members of Parliament had of Europe it is instructive to note that the term 'Europe' appears neither in the extracts quoted nor in the record of the full debate. Instead, the term 'Christendom' is used as the collective noun to describe the various European countries. Christendom in this sense is more than just a geographical expression. It implies a set of cultural norms held by the constituent countries, an implication made more potent by the presence of the 'heathen' Turkish Empire west of Constantinople. The term 'Europe' was by no means unknown. Massinger, for example, in his *Maid of Honour* (1632) referred to England as 'The Empress of the European Isles'. But 'Christendom' tended to be more common.

In the aftermath of the Reformation, religion, above all else, coloured the attitudes of Members of Parliament to the different states in Europe. Foreign policy was seen explicitly, if somewhat naively, in terms of a Catholic world and a Protestant world, rather like the present-day ideological polarization between the 'free world' and the 'communist world'. Hostility to Catholicism and Spanish efforts to close the West Indies to English shipping combined to make a bogey of Spain. Sympathy for Protestantism also perhaps clouded members' eyes to the emergence of the Dutch as a serious commercial rival.

Thus far in discussing English interest in Europe, we have been looking at the attitudes and perceptions of Members of Parliament and I need hardly remind you that MPs were a small and select body. How typical were they of their fellow-countrymen and women? It is to this broader question that we must now turn.

EXERCISE

What did 'Europe' mean to the men and women of early Stuart England? (Suggestion. Don't treat this as a strictly historical question. Use your imagination, be speculative and, while drawing on previous background information, and your reading of the course so far, don't worry if your ideas run ahead of your factual knowledge.)

DISCUSSION

1 There are different ways of approaching this question. I began by drawing a distinction between those people who had direct personal experience of European countries and those who had not. In the first category, there were the following groups:

(a) *Ambassadors, envoys and their entourages* Although a permanent diplomatic services was a thing of the future, English embassies were maintained in some style in Paris, Madrid and the Hague; permanent residents at various times, were placed in Venice, Turin, Brussels and Constantinople; and, in the major European ports, consuls, usually merchants, represented English interests. In addition, royal initiatives in European affairs called for special envoys to European courts.

Sir Dudley Digges who played a prominent role in the 1621 parliamentary debates on foreign policy had served on diplomatic missions both to the Netherlands and to Russia. Sir Henry Wotton, author of the influential *The Elements of Architecture* (1624) acquired his knowledge of Palladian architecture during his twenty years as English ambassador in Venice. Thomas Howard, Earl of Arundel, bibliophile and patron of the arts, was able to combine his antiquarian interests with embassies to the Netherlands and Germany in the 1630s. Buckingham and Charles, supposedly incognito, went to Madrid in 1623 on James I's behalf – a mission that was exceptional only because it included the heir to the throne.

Embassies and missions involved not just the ambassador or envoy in question but, variously, their families, secretaries, servants, chaplains and hangers-on and brought a select if somewhat disparate collection of Englishmen and women into direct contact with the wider world across the English Channel.

(b) *Merchants, factors and seamen*   Foreign trade also brought Englishmen into contact with Europe both directly and indirectly. Many merchants were really home-based capitalists investing in overseas trade but they often relied on English factors and English shippers to handle their goods. Ships from the west country ports plied a regular trade with France and Spain while those from the east coast ports concentrated on the Low Countries and the Baltic. London shipping could be found in any major port in Europe. From Riga to Barcelona expatriate Englishmen lived in separate merchant communities. The process of trade is not contained by ideological boundaries. English merchants domiciled abroad may well have found their national prejudice confirmed, or their religious views strengthened through living in an alien world, but they were engaged in commercial dealings which may also have tempered their attitude to the country in question. In piecing together an English view of Europe, the business perspective – commercial advantage and economic self-interest – needs to be borne in mind.

(c) *Private travellers*   We have so far considered the English who travelled in Europe in their capacity as servants of the state or for the purposes of trade but the early seventeenth century saw a marked increase in the amount of private travel to Europe. If Spain and Scandinavia were, except for merchants, largely off the beaten track and Germany was closed by war between 1618 and 1648, the Low Countries were open and near at hand. William Brereton, later a general on the parliamentarian side in the civil war, kept a diary of his visits to the United Provinces in 1634–5 and was one of a number of English travellers who admired the tidy cities and the industrious nature of the Dutch people.

Despite the commercial and religious links between England and the United Provinces, it was the cultural attractions of France and Italy that drew the wealthy English travellers – particularly the sons of the well-to-do gentry. 'I went abroad,' wrote William Tumbrull, 'and spent two years in France and Italy where I learned little besides the languages partly from my youth and the warmth of my temper, partly from laziness and debauchery.' The intention, at least, was clear. Visits to France and Italy were seen as a means of rounding off a young man's education. Inigo Jones in the retinue of Thomas Howard, Earl of Arundel, had something of an Italian apprenticeship before embarking on his architectural career in England. William Harvey pursued his medical studies in Padua. Milton travelled extensively in Italy in the late 1630s, as did John Evelyn in the early 1640s. Thomas Hobbes spent many years acting as tutor to the sons of the nobility and gentry on cultural pilgrimage in France and Italy. The Grand Tour, evidently, had its origins in the early seventeenth century.

In France, the English sons of a largely Protestant aristocracy and gentry could be found at language schools in the major Catholic cities, as well as in such Huguenot towns as Blois or Saumur, in the households of the nobility, at riding schools, and even dancing academies, in Paris and on the fringes of the French court.

From at least the 1630s, English travellers to Italy were able to follow a well-trodden route leading from Marseilles to the western coast of Italy on to Rome and Naples and then across to the eastern coast, with Venice the ultimate destination. They saw for themselves the classical heritage of the Roman world and were able to admire the art and architecture of post-Renaissance Italian cities. As relationships between the English Court and the Papacy grew easier, Rome increasingly became the most important stage in this itinerary and the English College of Jesuits often acted as host to English travellers, Protestant and Catholic alike.

Exposure to French fashions, Italian art and the influence of the Jesuits must have given impressionable young Englishmen something of a culture-shock. Many, like Milton, returned with their Protestant beliefs intact, even

The new tydings out of Italie are not yet com.

Out of Weenen, the 6 November.

THe French Ambaſſadour hath cauſed the Earle of Dampier to be buried ſtately at Preſburg. In the meane vvhile hath Bethlem Gabor cited all the Hungeriſh States, to com together at Preſburg the 5. of this preſent, to diſcourſe aboute the Crovvning & other cauſes concerning the ſame Kingdom.

The Hungatians continue vvith roveing againſt theſe Lands. In like manner thoſe of Moravia, vvhich are fallen uppon the Coſackes yeſter night by Hotleyn, ſet them on fire, and ſlaine many dead, the reſt vvill revenge the ſame.

Heere is certaine nevves com, that the Crabats, as alſo the Lord Budean, are fallen unto Betlem Gabor.

The Emperour ſends the Earle of Altheim, as Ambaſſadour to Crackovv in Polen, to appeare uppon the ſame meeting-day.

Novv comes tidings, that Betlem Gabor is at Thurna, there doe gather to gether great ſtore of States.

The Emper. Maj. bath appoynted heere a meeting-day uppon the 1. of Decemb. thereupon ſhould appare the 4. Proclaimed States. The appoynted taxing ſhall bring up a great ſom of money.

Out of Prage, the 5 of November.

Three dayes agone are paſſed by, 2 mile from this Cittie 6000 Hungarians (choſen out Soldiers) under the General Rediſerens, vvhich are gon to our Head-camp, & the Enimie lieth yet near unto ours by Rackonits, though the crie goeth, that the enimie cauſed all his might to com togither, to com this vvayes againſt Prage, if that comes to paſſe, it ſhall not run of vvithout blovves, the vvhich might be revealed vvithin ſevv dayes.

It coutinues, that in the Satſer Crais are gathered togither 10000 Contrie-men, moſt high-dutch-men, againſt Meitlen, & no Bohemians, they vvill help the King, to drive the enimie out of the Land. In like manner ſom certaine 1000 Contrie-men rebel in the LentmaritſcherCrais, but it is feared that thoſe Countriè-men are ſtarred up, through practiſe of the Adverſarie, that the enimie in the meane vvhile might com to Prage. Wee underſtand, that Bucquoy hath not been in the Camp, but by the Duke of Saxen ſom certaine dayes, therefore vve are to looke to our ſelves, for feare of Trecherie. And it is thonght that the Emperour vvill leave Auſtria to the Hungorians, & ſee to effect his intention only uppon Praghe.

Out of Ceuln, the 21. Novemb.

Writing from Marpurg in Heſſen, that the Earle of the ſame Land, doth cauſe the foreſaid Cittie to be ſtrongly fortified, there on doe vvorke many 100 men dayly, and there is muſtered in the Earleſhip Zigenheym not long ſince 1. Governement of foote-men, & 6. Corners of horſe-men, the foote-men are ſent to Marpurg & Rijnfels. But the horſe-men are lodged in the Villages about the Cittie, & thereafter are alſo muſtered the Duke of Saxen Lauvvenburgs Governement in Tries-Zigenheym, novv further vvhere they ſhallbe laid & uſed, is yet unknovvn. The ſames Brothers Governement, there quarter is laid by Caſſel, the Souldiers vvhich are taken on about Hamburg, Lubeck, in the Dukeſhip of Holſteen, & Meckelenburg, ſhould alſo be muſtered about Caſſel, & be uſed vvhere neede ſhall require.

Since the laſt vve cannot enquire, that there is any thing of any importaunce paſſed betvvixt the Marquis Spinola & the Vnited Princes. We underſtand that the foreſaid Spinola vvil lay his Souldiers in Garniſſon vvith the firſt, & deale them unto divers places, on part to Oppenheym, Altzey, Ingelheym & Cruiſinach, the other part at Summeren & Bacharacht, the ſpeech goeth that there ſhalbe layed vvith in Ments a good Company in Garniſſon.

The Biſhop at Halberſtadt, Duke Chriſtiaen at Bruynſvvyck, doth cauſe to be taken on 2000 Muſquetters, to ſend to the Vnited Princes.

Heere is tydings, that betvveen the King of Bohemia & the Emperours ſolke hath beene a great Battel about Prage, but becauſe there is different vvriting & ſpeaking thereuppon, ſo cannot for this time any certainety thereof be vvritten, but muſt vvayte for the next Poſt. As alſo of the Cittie Pilſen, vvhich the Earle of Manſvelt (ſo the ſpeech goeth) ſhonld have delivered into the Emperours hands.

From Cadan in Bohemia, 4 mile from Raconits, the 12. November.

From Solts is certaine adviſe that the Emperours folk have made them ſelves vvith all theire might out of theire Camp, & taken their vvay to vvards Praghe, like as they vveare then com to the long mile, but as the King underſtand ſuch, he is broken up vvith his armey, and com to the lóg mile beforen the enimie, vvhere they have had a very ſtrong Battelle & on both ſides more then 6000 men ſlaine, though moſt on the Kings ſide, alſo hath the enimie gotten of the King ſom peeces of Ordenuaunce and vvaggens vvith amunitie, ſo that the King muſt retire back to Praghe, and the enimie to the Weiſſenberg, there he lies yet and roves from thence to the Leut Maritſcher Crais unto Brix,

Figure 5 (continued on p 39)   Pages of the first newspaper to be printed in English, published by Pieter van den Keere, Amsterdam, dated 2 December 1620. (Reproduced by permission of the British Library Board.)

strengthened; some no doubt were converted to the Catholic faith and stayed behind, but all must have been forced to re-examine their values in the light of continental experience and, in so doing, see things European with new eyes.

(d) *Religious refugees*   If most English people viewed the Catholic mainland of Europe with an aggressive prejudice, there was a minority which fixed its sights on the return of their country to the Catholic faith. For the deeply-committed recusants the Jesuit schools at St Omer, Douai and Liège and the monastic communities at Cambrai, Gravelines and Dunkirk must have symbolized hope for the future. For some, the pull was even stronger hath taken in, Trebnits, Pielan & Dux, also laid folk upon Leutmarischer Slainer, and Launer passages, that the Passage upon Prage is wholy taken avvay, and this day is com heere in a certain Person that brings tydinghs unto our Magiftrat, that betvvixt Sonnevveid and Patronit, vvhere the enimie hath lien are found som certaine 1000 dead Bodies, & on the other side there King lay also som certaine 1000. dead bodies, vvhat is com to passe betvvixt both vve shal shortly heare.

Out of Amberghe, in the Vpper-Pallatine, the 17. dito.

Here hath beene a greate crie, that the Duke of Beyeren should have taken in Praghe, and beaten our King out of the fielde, but is not certaine, for the Carle of Solms vvrites out of Waltfaxfen of the 14 of this present, that the Duke of Beyeren vvas broken up with his camp very ftil. & marched in al haft to Prage, though they had left fom 100 men vvhich lay in theire quarter foom houres, vvhich made fires there in, that on vvoulde not have thought but that the vvhole Armay had layen there ftill, but as ours underftood that they vveregon follovved they them prefently, though the Beyerens vveid com to Weiffenberge before but the 8 of this present have ours fett uppon the Beyerens by force, and fought the vvhole day rogither, that on both fides are flaine aboute 8000 men, and very many fhould be huit. Our King, vvith the Lord General the Earle of Hohenlo, also the vvhole army are vvith in Prage, & the Duke of Beyeren uppon the Weyffenbergh & Stern; vve hoope that they shall shortly be driven from thence. Whatfurther is done betvvixt them, vve look for every houre to enquire further thereof & it feemes none can com from Prage, becaufe the paffages are every vvhere fhut.

Out of Ceulen, the 24 of November.

Letters out of Neurenburghe of the 20 of this prefent, make mention, that they had advife from the Borders of Bohemia, that there had beene a very great Battel by Prage, betvveen the King & the Duke of Beyeren, & many 1000. flaine on both fides, but that the Duke of Beyeren fhould have any folke vvith in Prage, is yet uncertaine, there uppon under the Merchants vvith in Neurenberge are laid many 100. Florins that the Emperour, nor the Duke of Beyeren have no folke vvith in Prage. The caufe that here comes no certainty thereof, is this; That all paffages ate fo befet, & fo dangerous to travaile, that it is to vvondered at, & not enough to be vvritte of, vvhat roveing, fpoyling and killing is done dayly uppon all vvayes.

Vppon the Schanfe Priefts cap is ftrongly buileed, & buy dayly much vvood lime & ftone, to make houfes there upon, and fo provide them felves for the vvhole vvinter. And are not long fince in the night 500 Souldiers paffed by Dure out of Gulik, fo the fpeech goeth, there meaning fhoulde be to build a nievv Schanfe by Flammerfheym, to take avvay the paffage from the Marquis Spinola.

Imprinted at Amfterdam by George Vefeler, Ao. 1620. The 2. of December.
And are to be foulde by Petrus Keerius, dvvelling in the Calverftreete, in the uncertaine time.

and throughout the reigns of James I and Charles I a steady trickle of Catholics crossed the Channel to France and the Low Countries. At one seminary alone, the Jesuit school at St Omer, there were two hundred English students on the roll in 1635. Without these schools and seminaries there was no means of providing English Catholics with native priests. Although such concentrations of exiles did not constitute a prima facie threat to English security they, without doubt, coloured English attitudes towards the host countries and especially France where the Protestant Huguenots became victims of a policy of state suppression.

But religious refugees were by no means all Catholic. From the 1590s Protestant separatist congregations settled in the Netherlands and the greater religious tolerance of Dutch society began to exert even stronger appeal for the separatists as Laudian religious policies began to bite.

(e) *Military volunteers, mercenaries and political exiles*   Some English Catholics joined the Spanish forces of occupation in the Low Countries. Some English Protestants volunteered for service in the Dutch army. But in the main the breakdown of service in continental armies does not appear to be expressly on religious lines. Mercenaries gravitate to the highest bidder. English mercenaries (and Scots and Irish too) served in the armies of all the major European powers. Ben Jonson saw active service in the Netherlands. Sir John Suckling, the poet, fought with Gustavus Adolphus. Sydenham Poyntz, later general of the parliamentary Northern Association kept a diary of his military experiences abroad.

The Thirty Years' War provided great opportunities for career soldiers and the experience of Englishmen in continental armies was initially crucial in the civil war. J. R. Jones tells us that the soldiers who had served in the Dutch army 'formed the most articulate and vehement group expressing Protestant views on foreign affairs'. Precisely how the experience of continental warfare affected the attitudes of English soldiers must be a matter for speculation but it is not to be under-estimated simply because it can't be measured.

Exigencies arising from the civil war in England meant self-imposed exile for some Englishmen. Writers and poets like Marvell, Waller, Lovelace and Davenant variously spent time in France and their direct acquaintance with French literature subsequently affected Restoration literary developments in England. Sir Roger Pratt, the gentleman architect, whose work was something of a synthesis of French, Dutch and Italian styles, was another exile whose influence on the Restoration scene was quite marked. Thomas Hobbes lived in Europe for most of the 1640s and regarded his return to England in 1651 as something of a gamble. Another 'gambler', Charles II, spent much of his time in exile in France, though at the last possible moment he was shrewd enough to remove himself to the United Provinces, thus enabling his return to England to be launched from an impeccably Protestant base.

2 If first-hand experience of Europe in the early seventeenth century was much greater than we often realize, it is also true to say that the vast majority of English nationals never went abroad. How did they obtain information about events in Europe? What did they think and feel about European issues?

These questions lead us into a consideration of the role of newspapers, the theatre, travel writing and the presence of foreign refugees in England. The record is scanty but as far as London and the major towns are concerned, it would be quite untrue to conclude that this meant general apathy or popular indifference to European affairs. How far images of Europe penetrated into rural England is perhaps another matter, though the diaries of country parsons like Josselin and Rous are littered with references to events in Europe.

(a) Censorship was a feature of seventeenth-century English political and social life. We are reminded in *C of R*, p 83, that until 1641 and again after 1660, the publication of home news was a legal offence and all imported foreign books were subject to episcopal censorship. Foreign news, however, did manage to reach England. From 1620, weekly English news-sheets or corantos were produced in Holland, principally Amsterdam, and sold on the streets of London and the major provincial cities (see *Figure 5*). In 1621 James I managed to persuade the States General to ban the export of corantos to England but the ban was never enforced. The lead given by these Dutch newspapers was quickly followed by such London printers as Nathaniel Butter and Nicholas Bourne who, from 1622 onwards, jointly produced a weekly newsbook on European affairs for a public thirsty for information about the ups and downs of the Thirty Years' War (see *Figure 6*). Despite cynics like Abraham Holland,

> But to behold the walls
> Buttered with weekly news composed in Pauls

these newsbooks proved to be popular in London and elsewhere. When, from 1632, they were proscribed, corantos printed in Amsterdam were smuggled into England in considerable numbers in order to satisfy the popular appetite for foreign news.

(b) The theatre, too, was affected by censorship, though the censor was not always a match for dramatists skilled at handling allusion and metaphor. The way that the popular London theatre mediated European stereotypes is discussed by Margot Heinemann in Block 2 'Middleton's *Women Beware Women*'.

(c) Published accounts of the travels of Englishmen in Europe also served to disseminate European stereotypes. Fynes Moryson (1566–1630), Thomas Coryate (1579–1617) and William Lithgow (1582–1645) made notable contributions to the genre of travel writing. For example Coryate's *Crudities* – an account of a European tour through France, Northern Italy, Venice, Ger-

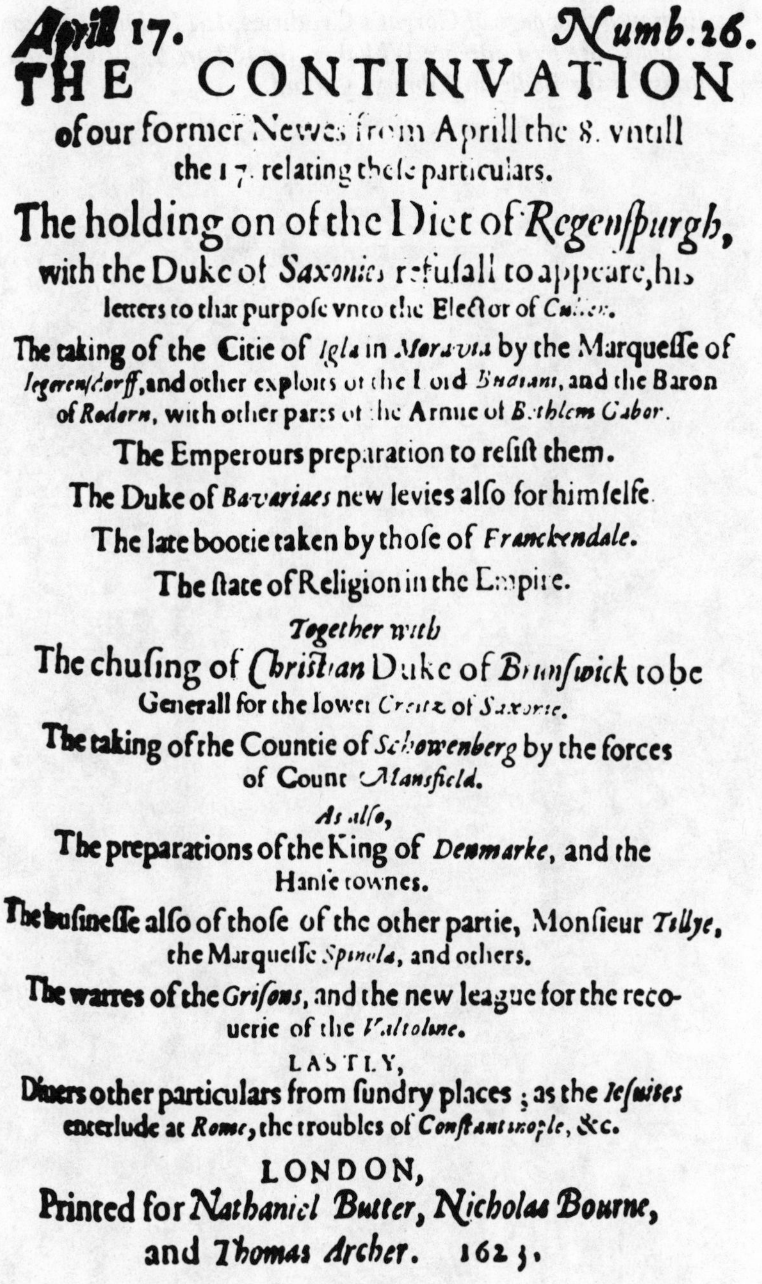

Aprill 17.   **Numb.26.**

THE CONTINVATION

of our former Newes from Aprill the 8. vntill
the 17. relating thefe particulars.

The holding on of the Diet of *Regenspurgh*,
with the Duke of *Saxonies* refufall to appeare, his
letters to that purpofe vnto the Elector of *Culcn*.

The taking of the Citie of *Igla* in *Morauia* by the Marqueffe of
Iegeren/dorff, and other exploits of the Lord *Bndiani*, and the Baron
of *Rodern*, with other parts of the Arnue of *Bethlem Gabor*.

The Emperours preparation to refift them.

The Duke of *Bavariaes* new levies alfo for himfelfe.

The late bootie taken by thofe of *Franckendale*.

The ftate of Religion in the Empire.

Together with

The chufing of *Chriftian* Duke of *Brunfwick* to be
Generall for the lower *Creitz* of *Saxonie*.

The taking of the Countie of *Schowenberg* by the forces
of Count *Mansfield*.

As alfo,

The preparations of the King of *Denmarke*, and the
Hanfe townes.

The bufineffe alfo of thofe of the other partie, Monfieur *Tillye*,
the Marqueffe *Spinola*, and others.

The warres of the *Grifons*, and the new league for the reco-
uerie of the *Valtoline*.

LASTLY,

Divers other particulars from fundry places ; as the *Iefuites*
enterlude at *Rome*, the troubles of *Conftantinople*, &c.

LONDON,
Printed for *Nathaniel Butter*, *Nicholas Bourne*,
and *Thomas Archer*.   1623.

Figure 6   The title page of a 24-page coranto, The Continuation of our former
newes, *Number 26, 8–17 April 1623. (Reproduced by permission of the British
Library Board.)*

many and the United Provinces and published in London in 1611 proved to
be very popular. His impressions of such things as the filthy streets of Paris,
the shocking behaviour of Venetian courtesans and the German penchant for
Rhenish wine must have influenced the attitudes of those who could not see
and experience Europe for themselves.

(d)   In their different ways, foreign refugees brought England into closer
touch with the continent. At one extreme, the presence of religious exiles in
London and the east coast towns reinforced the view that Europe was a
pernicious place of papists. At the other, foreign artists put the English Court
into the mainstream of European art. Court painting was dominated by
foreign artists – Mytens (*c.* 1590–1647), Van Dyck (1599–1641) and Rubens
(1577–1640) in the time of James I and Charles I; Lely (1618–80) and Kneller

Figure 7   Engraved title page of Coryat's Crudities, *1611. The explanatory coup-
lets A, B, C and G are by Laurence Whitaker, the rest are by Ben Jonson. (Reproduced by courtesy of the Bodleian Library, Oxford.)*

An explication of the emblemes of the frontispice

A   First, th'Author here glutteth Sea, Haddocke and Whiting
     With spuing, and after the world with his writing.

B   Though our Author for's Venerie felt no whips smart,
     Yet see here he rides in a Picardie Cart.

C   His love to strange horses he sorteth out prettilie,
     He rides them in France, and lies with them in Italie.

D   Here up the Alpes (not so plaine as to Dunstable)
     Hee's carried like a Cripple, from Constable to Constable.

E A Punke here pelts him with egs. How so?
   For he did but kisse her, and so let her go.

F Religiously here he bids, row from the stewes,
   He will expiate this sinne with converting the Jewes.

G Thy Cortizan clipt thee, ware Tom, I advise thee,
   And flie from the Jewes, lest they circumcise thee.

H Here, by a Boore too, hee's like to be beaten,
   For Grapes he had gather'd before they were eaten.

I Old Hat here, torne Hose, with Shoes full of gravell,
   And louse-dropping Case, are the Armes of his travell.

K Here, finer then comming from his Punke you him see,
   ★F. shews what he was, K. what he will bee.

L Here France, and Italy both to him shed
   Their hornes, and Germany pukes on his head.

M And here he disdain'd not, in a forraine land,
   To lie at Livory, while the Horses did stand.

N But here, neither trusting his hands, nor his legs,
   Beeing in feare to be rob'd, he most learnedly begs.

★Not meaning by F. and K. as the vulgar may peevishly and wittingly mistake, but that he was then comming from his Courtesan a Freshman, and now, having seen their fashions, and written a description of them, he will shortly be reputed a knowing, proper, and well traveld scholer, as by his starch'd beard and printed ruffe may be as properly insinuated.

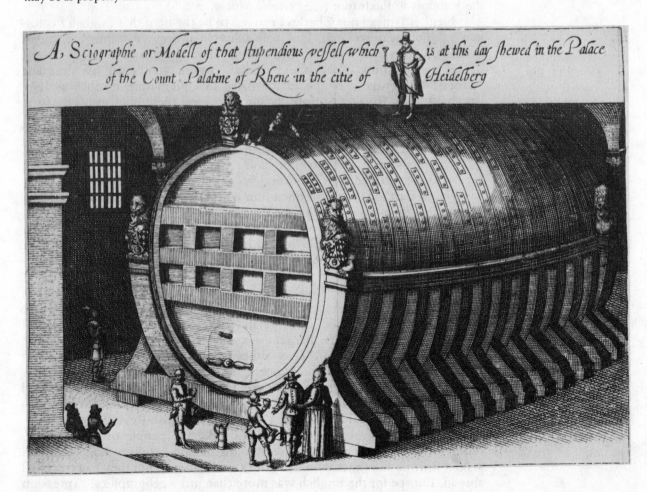

Figure 8 Coryat on top of the great tun of Heidelberg. (Engraving by W. Hole from Coryat's Crudities, *1611.)*

(1646–1723) after the Restoration. Wenceslaus Hollar (1607–77), noted for his topographical prints and his etchings of Van Dyck's portraiture, came from Bohemia and found his way to England in the retinue of Thomas Howard, Earl of Arundel. Isaac de Caius, responsible for the Franco–Flemish baroque style of Wilton House, was a Gascon (see Television programme 2).

3 A concept of 'Europe' must have entered popular consciousness. It must have reinforced an English public opinion largely and by now traditionally anti-Catholic, anti-Spanish and anti-papal. Throughout the 1620s and 1630s there was substantial popular sympathy for the Protestant cause in Europe. The English public took a partisan interest in the fortunes of Frederick, the Elector Palatine, son-in-law of James I and a Protestant prince. Frederick, who had accepted the crown of Bohemia against his father-in-law's advice, found himself labouring against an alliance between Spain and the Empire which succeeded in driving him, not just from Bohemia, but from the Palatinate as well. Aid for the Palatinate, as we have seen from the Commons Debates of 1621, became a subject of deep concern. We will return to this in the next section.

Nearer home the suppression of the Huguenots by the French crown constituted something of a *cause célèbre*. English seamen mutinied against the devious Buckingham when they got wind of an English plan to assist the French king against the Huguenots of La Rochelle. Milton's indictment of Charles I's alliance with France as a 'treacherous and antichristian war against the poor protestants of La Rochelle' gave form to popular sentiment. Milton continued to act as an informal spokesman for the Protestant cause in Europe embracing Scottish Presbyterians, Dutch Calvinists, and French Huguenots – or the 'Protestant International' as it has been called – and the force of his contribution can be gauged by the bitter condemnation of the massacre of the Vaudois in Piedmont (see *Portable Milton*, p 225).

Neither James I nor Charles I proved to be the hero that English Protestant opinion was seeking. This role fell to Gustavus Adolphus, King of Sweden, who was lionized in the English language press and in the letters, diaries and common-place books of the English gentry for his dramatic victories in Germany in the early 1630s. His premature death was long lamented. John Rous, a Suffolk parson, recorded these lines in his diary in 1633:

> Can Christendom's great champion sink away
> Thus silently into a bed of clay?
> Can such a Monarch die, and yet not have
> An Earthquake for to open him a grave?
> Did there no meteor fright the Universe
> Nor Comet hold a torch unto his hearse?
> Was there no clap of Thunder heard, to tell
> All Christendom their loss, and ring his knell?

In this atmosphere, English Protestant opinion viewed the English recusants with deep suspicion. The English Catholics were seen as people who owed their allegiance to Rome and were regarded as pro-Spanish and perhaps pro-French in the bargain – a cancer in the body politic. Crude stereotyping leads to absurd over-simplification. Emotional attachment to the Catholic faith need not necessarily lead to involvement in a Catholic crusade in England and Europe. It was perhaps 'the immense shadow and not the substance of Catholicism which frightened protestants' (Robin Clifton, 'The Popular Fear of Catholics during the English Revolution').

In considering the meaning of 'Europe' for people of seventeenth-century England, I began by drawing a distinction between those who had visited Europe and those who had not. Yet whether or not they had travelled abroad, Europe for the English was more than just a geographical expression as the frequent use of the term Christendom implies. Religious attitudes in

Figure 9 Matthaus Merian the Elder, Gustavus Adolphus in his Polish coat. *This was a scarlet cloak with silver embroidery which he wore on his triumphant entry into Frankfurt in November 1631. (Skokloster Castle, Sweden. Photograph by courtesy of Svenska Porträttarkivet, Nationalmuseum, Stockholm.)*

particular coloured people's perceptions, and different Englishmen and women saw Rome, France, Spain, the Dutch Republic and the Habsburg Empire differently according to their beliefs. But jostling this religious perspective, sometimes sharpening it, sometimes obscuring it, were commercial interests, war experiences, cultural pursuits, diplomatic activities, newspaper reports, theatrical caricature, travel writing, foreign refugees, patriotic aspirations and popular prejudice – images anyway which would have been fragmented by the class divisions of seventeenth-century English society. Although dominant attitudes can be picked out, 'Europe' meant different things to different English people in this period and is a more complex concept than it first appears.

3 English policy towards Europe 1618–1640

Thus far in discussing the English prospect of Europe, we have talked about different images, attitudes and perceptions. In talking about English policy towards Europe before 1640, we are talking essentially about the views of the Crown. The direction of foreign policy was a matter of royal prerogative. The royal and princely courts of Europe were the stage for the formalities of diplomatic relationships and the instrument of dynastic marriage underlined the personal role of royalty in foreign affairs. James I and Charles I, in theory at least, could make war and peace at will; in practice, the reality was somewhat different. In the short run they could not carry out ambitious overseas projects without obtaining parliamentary supply; and in the long term they could not afford to alienate persistently those people with a stake in the country. Tensions arising from differences over the conduct of foreign affairs ultimately contributed to the breakdown of political consensus.

The year 1618 is doubly inauspicious. At home it saw the execution of Sir Walter Ralegh. In Europe it saw the outbreak of the Thirty Years' War. The events leading to Ralegh's execution are sketched in *C of R* pp 31–2. Ralegh's death, according to a minister of state, 'moved the common sort of people to much remorse who all attributed his death to the desire His Majesty had to satisfy Spain'. This insensitive appeasement of Spain, 'a truckling to foreigners and Catholics' (Kenyon, *Stuart England,* p 73), also shocked the Puritan gentry and, though Ralegh was no Puritan, the manner of his death served to strengthen their resolve against James' policy. This in turn helped to widen the gap between Court and country, the theme of the next section.

The European war that broke out in 1618 lasted for more than a generation. Fighting was not incessant but ideological differences between Catholic and Protestant states pushed Europe into 'Cold War'. The European significance of the war has been hotly debated by recent historians but the domestic significance was readily grasped by an English contemporary. John Rushworth writing in 1659 intended to begin his account of the civil war in 1640 but found 'the difference between the King and Parliament forced me to a longer adventure' which went back to 1618 and the outbreak of war in the Palatinate, 'and how far the same concerned England and the oppressed Protestants in Germany'. (Preface to *Historical Collection* Vol. I 1618–29, London 1659; see also Hill *Milton and the English Revolution,* p 14.)

England did not play a decisive role in the Thirty Years' War (1618–48). In military affairs she was totally eclipsed by Sweden. Throughout the period she remained a second rate European power lagging behind first Spain, then France and even perhaps the Dutch. In the conduct of English foreign policy down to 1640, it is possible to identify three phases:

1 1618–22 with James I in personal control:

2 1622–8 with first Buckingham in ascendancy (to 1625) and then Charles and Buckingham in partnership;

3 1629–40 the personal rule of Charles I.

EXERCISE

Please read *C of R* pp 7–9, 29–34 and the Reader, article 4.

1 What do you think are the major trends in English foreign policy before 1640?

2 What are the main areas of disagreement between the Crown and its critics?

DISCUSSION

1 Despite shifts in foreign policy at least three general tendencies can be picked out:

(a) *Approchement with Spain* This was the cornerstone of James's policy – Anglo-Spanish understanding could pave the way for peace in Europe and bring about a negotiated settlement in the Palatinate; hence the importance that James attached to the Spanish marriage. Neither Buckingham, after 1624, nor Charles were as deeply committed to Spain. There was war against Spain, albeit half-hearted, in the mid–1620s and Charles in the mid–1630s showed his capacity for double-dealing over the Spanish Netherlands but taking the period as a whole and contrasting it with the previous half century, England and Spain moved closer together – at least on the formal level. By 1640 commercial and military co-operation between England and Spain in their dealings with the Spanish Netherlands was sufficiently real to disturb a substantial strand of parliamentary opinion.

(b)   *Accommodation with France*   France figured less prominently than Spain in the minds of English foreign policy makers. James showed a residual interest in the French Huguenots, Buckingham a wild inconsistency, Charles, after a flicker of concern in 1627–8, a tactless indifference. It would be an exaggeration to talk of pro-French policies in the 1630s but the ambitious scheming of Henrietta Maria and the influence she brought to bear at court appeared to tilt aspects of English policy in France's favour. Even some Protestants in the Queen's circle, like the Earl of Holland, were pro-French in the 1630s so not only Catholics, actual or concealed, looked favourably towards France.

(c)   *Deterioration in Anglo-Dutch relations*   As befitting the author of the *True Law of Free Monarchies* (see the Anthology, extract 10), James regarded the Dutch as rebels against properly constituted authority – in this case the King of Spain. Under Charles, as Anglo-Spanish understanding increased, with English ships handling Spanish troops and bullion destined for the Netherlands, so Anglo-Dutch relations worsened. English protestantism viewed such tendencies with chagrin and alarm, though this was tempered by elements who had personal knowledge of the lead the Dutch were establishing in overseas trade.

2   There were a number of separate but related criticisms of the foreign policy pursued by the English government. These included:

(a)   The failure of England to come out decisively in favour of the Protestant cause in Europe.

(b)   The apparent failure of the Crown to support a vigorous overseas commercial policy – a deficiency made even more galling by the solid support given by the Dutch government to its nationals.

(c)   The claims that the best interests of the country were being subverted by pro-Spanish, pro-French and pro-Catholic vested interests.

In exploring the dichotomy between government policy and parliamentary opposition over foreign affairs, Christopher Hill, echoing Gardiner, refers to 'two different foreign policies' (*C of R*, p 49). Strictly speaking this is misleading since, by definition, there is only one official foreign policy but it does serve to illustrate the point that by 1640, the divergence of views was beginning to generate on both sides a fateful coherence.

4   Court and Country

In the previous section, we touched on some of the differences between the King and his critics over the conduct of foreign affairs. Differences as strong, if not stronger, existed over domestic policy. The Petition of Right of 1628 (see Anthology, extract 13) listed a series of grievances, e.g. billeting, martial law, forced loans and imprisonment without trial, which touched the 'political nation' deeply; and the years of personal rule of Charles I (1629–40) which saw amongst other things, the abuses of monopolists, the outcry over Ship Money and Laudian innovation in church matters, widened the gulf between the crown and its critics (see *C of R* pp 57–62). Divergences of interest went much deeper than just differences of opinion over policies. The values, standards and morals of a royal court, 'more like Babylon than the New Jerusalem' (P. W. Thomas, Reader, extract 21), scandalized the godly and alienated many middle-of-the-roaders. This cultural rift gave a psychological dimension to the differences between the Crown and its critics. The antitheses between the 'Court' on the one hand, and the 'Country' on the other have been wittily amplified by Lawrence Stone:

> ... the Country was virtuous, the Court wicked; the Country was thrifty, the Court extravagant; the Country was honest, the Court corrupt; the Country was chaste and heterosexual, the Court promiscuous and homosexual; the Country was sober, the Court drunken; the Country was nationalist, the Court xenophile; the Country was healthy, the Court diseased; the Country was outspoken, the Court sycophantic; the Country was the defender of old ways and old liberties, the Court the promoter of administrative novelties and new tyrannical practices; the Country was solidly Protestant, even Puritan, the Court was deeply tainted by popish leanings.
>
> (Stone *The Causes of the English Revolution*, pp 105–6)

The dichotomy between 'Court' and 'Country' embracing moral, cultural and psychological divergencies, as well as political, economic and religious differences, has been used by some recent commentators as an organizational framework for advancing explanations of the breakdown in consensus that led to the civil war. Such divisions were not lost on contemporary opinion as you will see in the following exercise.

EXERCISE

What impressions do you get about the 'Court' and the 'Country' from the following extracts?

(a)   Say to the Court it glows
            and shines like rotten wood,
        Say to the Church it shows
            what's good, and doth no good.
        If Church and Court reply,
            then give them both the lie.

        (Sir Walter Ralegh, 'The Lie')

(b)   Thou art not, Penshurst, built to envious show
        Of touch or marble, nor can boast a row
        Of polished pillars, or a roof of gold;
        Thou hast no lantern, whereof tales are told,
        Or stair or courts but stand'st an ancient pile,
        And these grudged at, art reverenced the while . . .

        And though thy walls be of the country stone,
        They're reared with no man's ruin, no man's groan;
        There's none that dwell about them, wish them down . . .

        Thy lady's noble, fruitful, chaste withal;
        His children thy great lord may call his own
        A fortune, in this age, but rarely known . . .

        (Ben Jonson, 'To Penshurst')

(c)   I tell thee, I will have no more masquing; I will not buy a false and fleeting delight so dear: The merry madness of one hour shall not cost me the repentance of an age . . . I will no more of these superfluous excesses.

        (Ben Jonson, *Love Restored*)

DISCUSSION

Ralegh, not without good reason, is bitingly cynical about the Court. He conjures up an image of glistening surfaces and shining exteriors but something which is empty, hollow and rotten within. 'Shines like rotten wood' is a telling simile for the masque. (See below for an explanation of this theatrical genre.) In context the extract quoted from *Love Restored* is from the anti-masque sequence of the play designed to reinforce courtly superiority by parody. Out of context, it can be read as an indictment of the masque – costly, ephemeral and spurious – and by implication, of the Court itself. Penshurst, in contrast, is a different world – chaste, virtuous, humane, loyal and wholesome – an idealized country house set in rural arcadia. (You will find the complete poem in the Anthology, extract 16. You will find further examples of the genre of country house poems, in the radio programmes and on the cassettes.)

Although the Court under Charles I presented a less scandalous front to the world than it did in the licentious days of James I, it was seen as an arena in which 'popery, paintings and play acting' (P. W. Thomas, Reader, article 21) thrived, thereby causing anxiety and resentment in those outside the charmed circle. (See Margot Heinemann, Block 2 'Middleton's *Women Beware Women*'.) William Prynne captured these frustrations when he referred to developments at Court as a plot 'to seduce the King himself with Pictures, Antiquities, Images and other vanities brought from *Rome*'. Let's take a closer look at some of these strands.

The Court masque

The masque was a form of dramatic entertainment (at first amateur, later likely to be professional) which originally consisted of dancing and dumb-show but later included dialogue and song. The performers were masked and they enacted a more or less mythological or allegorical story amidst elaborate scenic effects. The genre had its origins in France and Italy, but was given an English significance through the combined talents of Ben Jonson and Inigo Jones. Masques were notoriously expensive to mount, calling for elaborate sets, complex stage machinery and exotic costume; and more often than not, they were given only a single performance at Court, though they were sometimes staged elsewhere. The underlying purpose of the masque was the 'ritual glorification of the monarch'. (Ashton, *The English Civil War*, p 71.) The masque is not so much political propaganda, since the action is played out within the closed world of the Court, but a re-assertion and re-affirmation of monarchical identity through the fusion of reality and illusion. To the country gentry, the masque came to be regarded as a symbol of the extravagance and immorality of the Court, perhaps made all the more powerful by the exclusive character of the Court itself.

Painting and architecture

To the modern eye, Charles I can be regarded as a discerning patron, employing some of the finest talents in Europe and building up an art collection that was the envy of even the most sophisticated of the European courts. Few contemporary Englishmen would have seen him in this light. The royal portraiture of Van Dyck smacked of inappropriate imperial grandeur, the Rubens ceiling in the Banqueting House at Whitehall an untimely transfiguration of monarchy and the architecture of Inigo Jones in Greenwich and Whitehall an unwanted Italianate importation. (For further elaboration, see 'Architecture and Society' in Block 2.) Drawing its inspiration from France, Italy and the Spanish Netherlands, the painting and architecture of the Caroline Court gave public expression to the cultural rift between itself and the country at large.

Figure 10   Anthony van Dyck, King Charles I on a white horse, *1633. An image of Stuart monarchy in the European style. (Royal Collection. Reproduced by gracious permission of Her Majesty the Queen.)*

Catholic influence at Court

This centred on Henrietta Maria who, openly professing her Catholicism, attracted a coterie of Catholic sympathizers to the Court. After the death of Buckingham, her influence over Charles I was particularly strong. She campaigned for the relaxation of the recusancy laws against Catholics and in 1637 even persuaded Charles to receive a papal agent at Court – an event seen by the largely Protestant country as something of a national betrayal. It is not perhaps surprising that Laudian religious policies were mistakenly seen by some as the thin edge of a Catholic wedge driven by the Court party. In truth, the Court was neither as pro-Catholic nor as degenerate as its severest critics made it out to be, but rumour mingled with fact to create a strained climate of opinion.

The concept of 'Country' is an important element in the ideology of opposition to the early Stuart kings. We have already seen in the previous

Figure 11   Anthony van Dyck, Queen Henrietta Maria. *For a different view of Henrietta Maria you may recall that Charles I's niece saw her as 'a small woman . . . with long skinny arms and teeth like defence works projecting from her mouth' (C of R, p 84). (Royal Collection, Windsor. Reproduced by gracious permission of Her Majesty the Queen.)*

exercise and in the quotations from Lawrence Stone, how the country stood for an ideal of moral superiority over a corrupt Court, and a particular life-style rooted in the English countryside. But there was also an institutional dimension to the concept of Country – quarter sessions and musters; the justice of the peace and the deputy lieutenant – which embraced local government and country administration. The inroads made into the power and influence of the nobility and country gentry through the exercise of the royal prerogative in the 1630s were seen by some as unwarranted intrusions into local affairs and further exacerbated the strains between the Crown and its opponents.

EXERCISE

What do you think are the limitations of such concepts as 'Court' and 'Country' in exploring tensions in seventeenth-century English society?

Figure 12   Peter Paul Rubens, Head of George Villiers, Duke of Buckingham, *c. 1625. (Graphische Sammlung Albertina, Vienna.)*

DISCUSSION

Obviously you will be in a better position to tackle this question at the end of the course than at the beginning. But you may already have noted that such terms, by their very use, can over-simplify differences and exaggerate a sense of dichotomy. You may also have suggested that terms such as 'Country' do not lend themselves to precise definition.

Brian Manning (Reader, article 10) takes the question of over-simplification further by showing the co-operation between country opposition and Court opposition against the policies of the King in the years 1640–2. Derek Hirst, in differentiating between the 'Country' as a positive ideology (a view taken by Trevor-Roper and Zagorin) and the 'Country' as loyalty to the local community (a view taken by Everitt and Morrill) makes the important point that the term 'Country' means different things to different commentators. (Hirst, 'Court, Country and Politics before 1629'.) This point is taken up again by Ann Hughes in Block 4.

It is tempting to accept the tenor of Lawrence Stone's conclusion that by the early seventeenth century 'England was experiencing all the tensions created by the development within a single society of two distinct cultures, cultures that were reflected in ideals, religion, art, literature, the theatre, dress, deportment and way of life' (*The Causes of the English Revolution 1529–1642*, p 106.) But you need to remember that Court and Country could not exist in self-contained worlds. Political, administrative and financial considerations alone brought very real inter-connections between them and it would be a mistake to impose too artificial a polarization on the processes at work in early seventeenth-century society. But it would also be a mistake to ignore a distinction that made sense to contemporaries – the identification of the Country with 'the maintenance of traditional standards' and the Court with 'cultural, political, religious and numerous other varieties of innovation' (Ashton, *The English Civil War*, p 42).

Charles I and his courtiers would have been equally at home in Paris or Madrid as they were in London. Indeed, the style of the Caroline Court suggests considerable continental influence. In the seventeenth century, the institution of the Court was a European phenomenon. But there was much more to the European Court than style, privilege and high culture. H. R. Trevor-Roper, in particular, has argued that the concept of 'Court' and 'Country' has a European validity in the seventeenth century. The Court is seen as 'a top-heavy superstructure' of bureaucrats, administrators, officials and hangers-on and an apparatus for social oppression. This superstructure was shaken and in some cases toppled in the revolutionary decade 1640–50. Investigations into the structural weaknesses of seventeenth-century European society and institutions have led some historians to the view that there was a 'general crisis of the seventeenth century'. It is to this issue that we now turn.

5   The general crisis of the seventeenth century

In 1643 Jeremiah Whittaker in a sermon to the House of Commons proclaimed: 'These are days of shaking . . . and this shaking is universal: the Palatinate, Bohemia, Germania, Catalonia, Portugal, Ireland, England'. Whittaker's tumultuous perceptions were by no means unique. In 1651, the Venetian ambassador to the court of Spain reported Admiral Blake's roguish remarks in Cadiz:

> . . . following the example afforded by London, all kingdoms will annihilate tyranny and become republics. England has done so already; France will follow in her wake; and as the natural gravity of the Spaniards rendered them somewhat slower in their operations, he gave them ten years for the revolution in their country.

Universal shaking, annihilation of tyranny, the spread of revolution – the language evokes images of a society in crisis. One of the major controversies in current historiography revolves around this question of crisis. Let us explore the concept of 'the general crisis of the seventeenth century' by looking at views of the leading contributors in the debate.

EXERCISE

Below you will find seven extracts which illustrate the wide range of views about the general crisis of the seventeenth century. These extracts are taken out of context from closely-argued and deeply-held positions. Don't be put off by unsubstantiated assertions – the extracts have been deliberately chosen to illustrate the conflict of opinion. You don't need a detailed knowledge of the events mentioned in the extracts in order to do the exercise. As far as France and the Dutch Republic is concerned internal developments are elaborated in the next section.

First of all I would like you to summarize in your own words what *each* of the extracts tells us about the question of seventeenth-century crisis. Then I would like you to make comparisons by noting extracts which reveal similar and contrasting views.

Extract 1

The causes, courses and results of these six revolutions (Catalonia, Portugal, Naples, England, France and the Netherlands) afford an admirable example of the infinite variety of history. Though contemporaneous, they were curiously little alike; their differences were far more remarkable than their similarities.

(R. B. Merriman, *Six Contemporaneous Revolutions*, p 89.)

Extract 2

... I wish to suggest that the European economy passed through a 'general crisis' during the seventeenth century, the last phase of the general transition from a feudal to a capitalist economy ... The seventeenth-century crisis thus differs from its predecessors in that it led to as fundamental a solution of the difficulties which had previously stood in the way of the triumph of capitalism as that system will permit. In the first part of this essay I propose to marshal some of the evidence for the existence of a general crisis, which is still disputed by some, and to suggest an explanation of it. In the second part, I propose to discuss some of the changes it produced, and how it was overcome. It is very probable that a great deal of historical work will be done on this subject and period in the next few years.

(E. J. Hobsbawm, 'The Crisis of the Seventeenth Century' in Aston *Crisis in Europe, 1550–1650*, pp 4–5.)

Extract 3

Such, as it seems to me, was the 'general crisis of the seventeenth century'. It was a crisis not of the constitution nor of the system of production, but of the State, or rather, of the relation of the State to society. Different countries found their way out of that crisis in different ways. In Spain the *ancien régime* survived: but it survived only as a disastrous, immobile burden on an impoverished country. Elsewhere in Holland, France and England, the crisis marked the end of an era: the jettison of a top-heavy superstructure, the return to responsible, mercantilist policy. For by the seventeenth century the Renaissance Courts had grown so great, had consumed so much in 'waste', and had sent their multiplying suckers so deep into the body of society, that they could only flourish for a limited time, and in a time, too, of expanding general prosperity. When that prosperity failed, the monstrous parasite was bound to falter. In this sense, the depression of the 1620s is perhaps no less important, as a historical turning-point, than the depression of 1929: though a temporary economic failure, it marked a lasting political change.

(H. R. Trevor-Roper, 'The General Crisis of the Seventeenth Century' in Aston *Crisis in Europe 1550–1650*, pp 94–5.)

Extract 4

For a long time, the seventeenth century lacked, so far as the whole of Europe and the whole of the century were concerned, a special resounding epithet to describe it. The situation has markedly altered ... Many new works of a wide scope have appeared together with new theories which endeavour to systematise the knowledge that has accumulated, arranging it in some kind of general pattern which will embrace all or most of the countries of Europe and reveal what it was that determined the common features (or at least the similarity) of the processes taking place in these countries. In these theories the seventeenth century figures as something special as a century of very acute contradiction, a century of economic, social and political crisis, of a *crise de conscience*. It has at last been given its descriptive epithet and become the century of 'general crisis' and of 'general revolution', the 'tragic century'.

Many of these conceptions are dubious and even quite unacceptable, in the first place the very idea of 'general crisis' and 'general revolution' – but they are interesting in that they try to penetrate deeply into the essence of events, to track down some sort of fundamental causes of those processes of outstanding importance which were common to all the countries of Europe.

(A. D. Lublinskaya, *French Absolutism*, p 4.)

Extract 5

. . . there is a real danger in the whole concept of a General Crisis, just as any covering explanation tends to be fallacious in detail. It is misleading to think that the long-term problems of European States were the same, for they were obviously not. England and Spain shared little in common in 1640 except for the same date for their revolutions; Moscow and Paris in 1648, Amsterdam and Stockholm in 1650, coincided in time rather than problem. It is one thing to look at the common difficulties shared by social classes in different countries, quite another to generalise from the very uneven development of European states to the existence of a particularly significant crisis. A turning point did, of course, exist, and the occasion was supplied by the economic difficulties of the decade 1640–50. In those years of fiscal instability and price inflation, of bad harvests and the beginnings of a trade recession, the accumulated problems of governments and the grievances of their subjects exploded in a continent-wide outburst of revolution.

(Henry Kamen, *The Iron Century*, p 330.)

Extract 6

What I will be trying to demonstrate is that Europe entered a new era very roughly during the middle third of the century and that the best indication of this profound transformation is the very different atmosphere that reigned in the succeeding decades. Between say, the early 1630s and the early 1670s (though it would be foolish to insist on crisp cut-off points in so far reaching a process) there was a change in direction more dramatic and decisive than any that occurred in a forty-year period between the beginnings of the Reformation and the French Revolution. And it is precisely by recognising how different Europe's situation was in the *aftermath* of these events than it had been during or immediately preceding the great shift that we can come to appreciate the extent of the alteration that had been wrought.

(Rabb, *The Struggle for Stability in Early Modern Europe*, pp 3–4.)

Extract 7

There is no way in which the 'Little Ice Age', the bad harvests of the late 1630s or even Ship Money can be shown to have caused the English Civil Wars. The same is true of all the major political crises of western Europe in these years: the Fronde, the revolts of Portugal, Catalonia and the British Isles, the confrontations in Holland and Sweden. In each of them, the cause is to be sought not in the social structure and economic situation of the populations at large, but in the innovative policies of their governments especially in the fields of finance and religion.

(G. Parker and L. M. Smith, *The General Crisis of the Seventeenth Century*, p 14.)

DISCUSSION

1 Merriman (Extract 1), the first historian to explore the cross currents of the revolts, uprisings and revolutions of the years 1640–50, sees a temporal but not a causal connection in the turbulence of the decade and implicitly rejects the concept of a general crisis.

2 Lublinskaya (Extract 4) also rejects the idea of a general crisis but has sympathy for any methodological approach which attempts to explore structural inter-relationships between the European states.

3 Kamen (Extract 5), for different reasons from Lublinskaya, sounds a warning about the validity of the concept of general crisis. But his 'turning point', a product of the fusion of the political and economic difficulties of the decade 1640–50 is suspiciously like the 'general crisis' of other commentators.

4 Hobsbawm (Extract 2) takes the view that there was a general crisis in the European economy in the seventeenth century and that this crisis marked the last phase in the transition from a feudal to a capitalist economy.

5 Trevor-Roper (Extract 3) also propounds the notion of general crisis but locates the problem not so much in the economy as in the relation of the State to society and in the machinations of over-bearing Renaissance courts. Parker and Smith (Extract 7) likewise see the policies of European governments rather than the social structure or the economic situation of European populations at the heart of the question.

6 Rabb (Extract 6) too, subscribes to the general crisis theory of the seventeenth century. But the issue is wider than political or economic considerations – for him the years 1630–70 saw a profound shift in the European conscience.

Overall these extracts point to a wide-ranging and unresolved debate in the historiography of the seventeenth century. Given more space I could have introduced you to various other contributors. The debate is complex, many-sided and, in all fairness, you will only appreciate the force of the arguments by a close reading of the contributions in full. Even then, along with Theodore K. Rabb's 'advanced students' you might come away 'with the impression that chaos reigns, that there is no way of reaching firm conclusions or imposing a coherent framework on so contentious a subject' (Rabb, *The Struggle for Stability in Early Modern Europe*, p vii). The risk is worth taking. Whatever side you take – or even if you stay on the sidelines – you will come to realize that the 'general crisis' debate has increased our understanding of the processes at work in European society in the seventeenth century. For this reason, the two remaining parts of this section are given over to a brief résumé of the historiography of the 'general crisis' question and a short consideration of the significance of the 'general crisis' issue for the history of seventeenth-century England.

The historiography of 'The general crisis of the seventeenth century'

The question of a 'general crisis of the seventeenth century' has been a live issue for the last twenty-five years or so and continues to arouse controversy. E. J. Hobsbawm opened up the question in 1954 in the historical journal *Past and Present*. Part of the introduction to Hobsbawm's piece has been quoted in Extract 2 (see above p 54). Following this statement of intent, Hobsbawm proceeded to deduce widespread economic deterioration in seventeenth-century Europe through a consideration of factors such as population trends, production, demand and markets. He rejected the notion that war, particularly the Thirty Years' War, caused the crisis; and, using a Marxist analytical framework, argued that the crisis was caused by hindrances and obstacles in the way of the development of capitalism, e.g. the feudal structure of society, the narrowness of the home market, the slackness in overseas and colonial markets. The resolution of the crisis came about by a redeployment of capital which led to modifications in the structure of European society and prepared the ground for industrialization. For Hobsbawm, then, the crisis was 'the broom that swept away the old and made way for the new' (Rabb, *The Struggle for Stability in Early Modern Europe,* p 18).

H. R. Trevor-Roper in 1959, also in an article in *Past and Present,* carried the torch forward. Part of his conclusion is given in Extract 3 (see above p 54). Trevor-Roper, no less than Hobsbawm, propounds the notion of a general crisis but he sees it in very different terms. Observing that the revolutions in the middle of the seventeenth century, 'have so many common features that they appear almost as a general revolution', he proceeds to investigate the character of this upheaval. He considers the intellectual background, the effects of war, the structural weaknesses of western monarchies, but finds in none of these features a sufficient explanation. He further rejects the Marxist identification of the seventeenth-century revolutions with bourgeois capitalist revolution (an equation made by Hobsbawm), as 'a mere *a priori* hypothesis'. So if it was neither a constitutional crisis nor a crisis of economic production what kind of crisis was it? Trevor-Roper answers the question as follows. It was something 'both wider and vaguer than this . . . a crisis in the relationship between society and the State' in which the dominant features were the rise of the Renaissance courts, the eclipse of the cities, the development of parasitic bureaucracies and the emergence of puritanism as the ideology of a counter-culture.

Trevor-Roper's piece stimulated a flurry of replies including contributions from Roland Mousnier, J. H. Elliott and Michael Roberts who argued that the Trevor-Roper thesis was not borne out by developments in France, Spain and Sweden respectively. All the above-mentioned articles, along with others bearing on the question, were published in *Crisis in Europe 1550–1650* (Aston, 1965). Since then the issues raised in the debate have been taken up in different ways in various general studies of the period. We have already referred to three of these in the previous exercise – A. D. Lublinskaya (1968); Henry Kamen (1971); and Theodore K. Rabb (1975). In 1978, a number of important articles written since the first appearance of *Crisis in Europe,* were brought together by David Parker and Lucy M. Smith under the title of *The General Crisis of the Seventeenth Century*. This includes, for example, an essay by Ruggiero Romano, the historian of European trade, on the theory of general economic downturn from around 1620. And so it goes on. Neither in specialist articles nor in general surveys can the concept of 'general crisis' now be ignored in interpretations of seventeenth-century European history.

'General crisis' and the history of seventeenth-century England

What is the significance of the theory of 'general crisis' for the history of seventeenth-century England and in particular the years 1640–60?

So far I've introduced you to a number of different interpretations of the nature of the 'general crisis':

(a)   a crisis in economic production;
(b)   a political crisis;
(c)   a crisis of the spirit;

and also to two different time periods to which the term has been applied:

(a)   1640–50: the revolutionary decade;
(b)   the seventeenth century as a whole.

In turn, this suggests that historians have not reached precise agreement on the meaning of the term 'crisis' itself. You may have already begun to make judgements about the merits of the respective arguments. You may have kept a completely open mind. You may even be thoroughly confused by the whole question – though I hope not! Whatever your stance, when you come to study later material in this course, you will have cause to reflect on the significance of the theory of 'general crisis'. This, as we have seen, is very much an open question. It seems to me, however, that you will at least need to take account of the following points:

1   Historians, in the main, now seem to be agreed that western and central European countries experienced some form of political and/or economic crisis during the seventeenth century.

2   Explanations as to what happened in England, in the period 1640–60 – a 'Great Rebellion', a 'Puritan Revolution', a 'Bourgeois Revolution' – are unlikely to be satisfactory if seen solely from an internal or domestic viewpoint.

3   As a corollary of 2 the response to and the outcome of crises in European states can be used to shed light on the precise nature of the crisis in England.

It is with this comparative point firmly in mind that we consider the significance of French and Dutch models of society for seventeenth-century English development.

6   Crisis in England: French and Dutch models of society

EXERCISE

The extract below is taken from the introduction to G. M. Trevelyan's *England under the Stuarts* which was first published in 1904 and went through nineteen editions by 1947.

> England has contributed many things good and bad to the history of the world. But of all her achievements, there is one, the most insular in origin and yet the most universal in effect. While Germany boasts her Reformation and France her Revolution, England can point to her dealings with the House of Stuart.
>
> . . . But the transference of sovereignty from Crown to Parliament was effected in direct antagonism to all continental tendencies. During the seventeenth century a despotic scheme of society and government was so firmly established in Europe, it would have been the sole successor of the mediaeval system.
>
> . . . But at this moment the English, unaware of their destiny and of their service, tenacious only of their rights, their religion and their interests, evolved a system of government which differed as completely from the new continental model as it did from the chartered anarchy of the Middle Ages.

How does Trevelyan characterize political developments in seventeenth-century Europe?

DISCUSSION

Trevelyan wears his prejudice and his insularity on his sleeve. England and Europe happily went their separate ways. In Europe, the absolutist monarchies were able to impose a 'despotic scheme of society and government' on their subjects, whereas in England the successful struggle for religious and civil liberty brought about a transfer of 'sovereignty from crown to parliament'.

Trevelyan invoked a 'continental model' of government of monolithic proportions. Contemporaries did not see it in quite such simplistic terms. In 1648 *Mercurius Pragmaticus,* the Royalist weekly journal, railed against 'the new fundamentals', attacking those tendencies which 'from a glorious Monarchy be translated into a Dutch model, from the subjection of a King to the arbitrary vassalage of a free state'. But with the exception of the United Provinces the trend in continental countries was towards absolute monarchy – a tendency which found its fullest expression in France. So we have two continental models of government and society – the French and the Dutch.

Before we consider the significance of these models, I would like you to think again about the different ways that images of France and the Dutch Republic impinged on English society. J. R. Jones, Reader, article 4, nicely charts the cross-currents of appeal. There was, as we have seen earlier, a certain ambivalence towards the Dutch. Ideological, religious and commercial links were strong but at the same time the interests of English political and economic élites were not served by the subversive literature coming off Dutch printing presses, by the commercially aggressive policy of the Dutch government, and by the skulduggery of Dutch merchants in overseas and colonial markets. Affinities with France tapped a different sectional interest. Many well-to-do gentry and aristocracy admired French culture, fashion and style of government, though as the long reign of Louis XIV (1643–1715) wore on, there was something of a volte-face in English opinion.

Few historians today would accept the isolationism of England from the continent implied by Trevelyan, though the extent to which English people consciously looked to Dutch republicanism and French absolutism as alternative models of English government and society is a more open question. In order to explore this aspect, we need first to outline some of the features of French and Dutch political development during the seventeenth century.

France

During the course of the seventeenth century, France replaced Spain as the major power in Europe. The French monarchy, as it emerged under Louis XIV became the prototype of absolute monarchy and the new royal palace of Versailles came to be regarded as 'the very symbol of absolutism'. (Kossmann, 'The Singularity of Absolutism'.)

Figure 13   Patel, Versailles in 1668. *(Musée de Versailles. Photograph by H. Roger-Viollet.)*

The French monarchy endured the double misfortune of consecutive minorities. Louis XIII was a boy of nine when he succeeded to the throne in 1610, and Louis XIV was five when he became King in 1643. The monarchy coped with various tax revolts and frequent peasant uprisings. It tackled head-on the question of the Huguenots and it responded to the demands of foreign wars. But the most serious internal problem it had to face was the Fronde. The period of the Fronde (1648–53) is a complex, involved and intriguing moment in French history. It had its ludicrous aspects – the very name is derived from a children's game of throwing stones at the carriages of the rich – but it represented a challenge to the organization of the mid-seventeenth century French state. There were various strands of discontent:

(a)   disaffection of sections of the nobility;

(b)   resistance of the *parlement* of Paris (the highest court in the land and a body with political ambitions, but a very different institution from the English parliament) to a vigorous policy of centralization under the crown;

(c)   provincial dissatisfaction with central tax and administrative agencies;

(d)   acute urban and rural poverty;

(e)   the almost universal dislike of Mazarin, the chief minister of the crown, and distrust of his military and foreign policy;

and 1648 was a year when revolution was in the air.

The *parlement* of Paris took the initiative and came forward with a programme of wholesale political reform. 'In spite of their declaration of loyalty to the King and absolute monarchy they were, in effect demanding constitutional monarchy if not a republic.' (Menna Prestwich, 'The Making of Absolute Monarchy 1559–1683'.) The government bought time with a policy of concession and compromise and the first phase of the crisis, the *Fronde parlementaire* gave way to the *Fronde princière* – the Fronde of the princes. For the best part of three years, factions of the highest French nobility caused the government acute embarrassment. Paris was occupied, the Court fled, and Bordeaux rose in revolt. The country teetered on the brink of civil war. But the government in the end rode out the storm and, by early 1653, felt strong enough to revoke all concessions. The disaffected nobility, the merchant and professional classes and the populace of Paris and Bordeaux had shown insufficient common interest to allow the development of a coherent anti-government strategy. After this *frisson*, the way was clear for the consolidation of royal absolutism – the exercise of power in the state unfettered by the restraints of representative assemblies.

At root, there were three essential components in the structure of French absolutism:

1   A centralized bureaucracy for the administration of royal policy. Under the two great servants of the seventeenth-century French state (Richelieu, 1585–1642, and Colbert, 1619–83), provincial autonomy was eroded, especially in the fields of justice and finance.

2   A system of taxation which could be operated with little or no recourse to parliamentary assemblies and which made the French monarchy the richest in western Europe.

3   A standing army – the importance of which was clearly spelt out by Colbert to a government official: 'You can be reassured and make the fact public that the King keeps prepared twenty leagues from Paris an army of twenty thousand men ready to march into any province where there is suspicion of a rising, in order to inflict exemplary punishment and to illustrate to the whole people the obedience they owe to His Majesty.'

Behind the façade, there was corruption, inefficiency and venality on a grand scale but absolutism as a system of government enabled the French monarchy to dominate the seventeenth-century European stage.

The Dutch Republic

The Dutch Republic consisted of the seven provinces of Holland, Zeeland, Utrecht, Friesland, Groningen, Overijsel and Gelderland. These provinces

Figure 14 The Dutch Republic in the seventeenth century. (Reproduced from J. L. Price (1974) Culture and society in the Dutch Republic during the seventeenth century, London, Batsford. By permission of the publishers.)

came together in resistance against Spanish control in the so-called Eighty Years' War which ended in 1648 with the formal recognition by Spain of Dutch independence. Given the very real differences between these provinces – differences which produced deep tensions in Dutch society – the union was nothing short of miraculous. Certainly without the Spanish presence, there would have been no union at all. Among the significant internal tensions were:

1 Provincial separatism versus centralization of government which, as we shall see, was reflected in constitutional arrangements.

2 The commercial interests of the merchant class of Holland and Zeeland versus the landed interests of the nobility and aristocracy of Gelderland, Overijsel and Groningen

3   The republicanism of the regents (the oligarchs who ruled the towns in Holland) versus the monarchical ambitions of the House of Orange.

4   Conflict in the Dutch reformed church between the Arminians (Remonstrants) backed by the regent oligarchy of Holland and the Gomarists (Contra-remonstrants) supported by the House of Orange. Disunity in religion was further compounded by the presence in the Republic of significant numbers of Catholics.

5   Cultural differences exemplified by the austerity of the Dutch School of painting at one extreme and the baroque art of the Orange Court at the other.

Each of the provinces of the Dutch Republic had its own separate government and strict limitations were imposed on the powers of the central government. 'Each province looked upon itself as sovereign and the Republic can be better regarded as an alliance of independent states than a single political unit' (Price, *Culture and Society in the Dutch Republic during the Seventeenth Century*, p 16).

The formal executive authority of the Republic resided in the Council of State, a body consisting of the stadtholders (an officer akin to a provincial governor) of the seven provinces, a number of provincial delegates and, until 1626, a representative of the English government. The Council of State was controlled by the States General, a body consisting of delegates from the provincial states, which was primarily concerned with the formulation of foreign and military policy. But the power of the States General itself was limited. Delegates were obliged to consult their own state governments for policy directives; within the States General each state had the right of veto; and taxation was a matter for provincial governments. There was a federal budget but no state could be compelled to pay towards a policy of which it disapproved. Much, then, was left in the hands of the local estates of the seven provinces and these varied considerably in character. Holland, for example, was controlled by the regents, the narrow mercantile élite of the major towns, whereas in Friesland merchants and the landed aristocracy sat side by side in an assembly elected by popular vote.

Of the seven provinces Holland was the most important by far. It provided more than half the military budget for the Republic and despite the checks and balances of the Dutch constitution, its voice had the strongest influence on the direction of Dutch policy. Not surprisingly, the pensionary of Holland – the spokesman of their deputation to the States General – came to play a major political role and amongst other things, assumed responsibility for the foreign policy of the confederation. This office was held by John of Oldenbarnevelt from 1586 until his execution in 1619 at the behest of Maurice Prince of Orange, stadtholder of Holland, Zeeland, Utrecht, Overijsel and Gelderland and commander-in-chief of the Dutch army. The differences between Oldenbarnevelt and Maurice provide different visions of the Republic. On the one hand, there is the commercial, pacific and pro-Arminian policy of the regents of Holland, on the other there is the dynastic, bellicose and pro-Gomarist policy of the House of Orange. The victory of the Orangist party in 1619 ushered in a period of dominance of the stadtholderate which was to last for thirty years.

The inner conflicts in Dutch society remained and these came to the surface again in the crisis of 1650. The crisis was sparked off by disagreement over the demobilization of troops following the peace treaty of 1648. William II who had become Stadtholder in 1647 (and who incidentally was married to Mary Stuart, the daughter of Charles I) found the peace policy unacceptable. He flirted with the idea of intervening in England on behalf of the Stuart cause and encouraged by French diplomacy, schemed for a resumption of the war with Spain. Holland found this war policy unacceptable. The Republic was deeply in debt, a pro-Stuart policy threatened relations with the new English government and war with Spain would continue to dissipate Dutch resources. Fears were also voiced over the monarchical ambitions of William II. Both sides stood firm, appealed to ancient prece-

Figure 15   Rembrandt, The Syndics, *the sampling officials (wardens) of the Amsterdam Drapers Guild, 1661–2. (Rijksmuseum, Amsterdam.)*

dents and prepared for the worst. Civil war was averted only by chance – the death of William II in November 1650.

The death of William II marked the turning point in the crisis and guaranteed that the Dutch revolution would be a peaceful one. The way was left clear for Holland to control the destinies of the Republic for a generation and the direction of Dutch policy fell to the pensionary of Holland, held by Johan de Witt (1652–70). Dutch domestic policy in these years has been characterized as 'mercantile, republican and tolerant' (Price, *Culture and Society in the Dutch Republic*, p. 27) but overseas Anglo-Dutch commercial rivalry proved stronger than republican sentiment and led to a series of naval wars between the Dutch Republic and England. The legacy of the naval wars though did not prevent a combination of English interests from turning to William of Orange as a way out of the crisis of 1688–9.

Crisis in England

The political crisis in England erupted with the calling of the Long Parliament in 1640. We have already seen how differences over foreign policy – *rapprochement* with Spain, the failure of England to rally to the cause of European protestantism, suspicions over France – widened the gap between the Crown and its critics. And how the cultural rift between Court and Country and the exclusion from office of large sections of the political nation contributed to the crisis. I would now like you to read *C of R* pp 38–47, 50–7 and consider the following question.

EXERCISE

How did disagreements over finance contribute to the constitutional crisis?

DISCUSSION

Government, even in the time of the Stuarts, was an expensive business – a reality made worse by price inflation. Tax assessments were low by comparison with some continental countries and the crown revenue was insufficient for the purposes of government – witness the steady sale of crown lands; if the King wanted to pursue even a moderately ambitious foreign policy royal revenue was woefully inadequate.

The Stuart kings resorted to residual devices within a powerful, though somewhat hazy, royal prerogative – feudal tenures, wardship (see the Anthology, extracts 19 and 20), sale of monopolies, sale of offices, purveyance, compulsory knighthood fines, ship money and forced loans – for the raising of non-parliamentary revenue. If such devices had been used sparingly or for the financing of policies broadly acceptable to the political nation, it is hard to see how a crisis could have developed. During the reigns of James I and increasingly during the reign of Charles I, the reverse was the case. Parliament, when it was sitting, and the law courts, were used as mechanisms for challenging the legitimacy of royal actions; though the partiality of the judicial bench was another matter (see the Anthology, extract 18). Whereas the Crown rested its case on the traditional and absolute nature of the royal prerogative, its opponents appealed to established practice, ancient precedent and the fundamental law (see the Anthology, extract 14). Impassioned appeals to history for the justification of a course of action suggest something of an impasse.

The Ship Money case (Anthology, extracts 21 and 22) raised matters of acute political significance. Angelo Correr, Venetian Ambassador in England, wrote to the Doge and Senate on 27 February 1637 as follows. 'Your Excellencies can easily understand the great consequences involved in this decision as at one stroke it roots out for ever the meeting of Parliament, and renders the King absolute and sovereign.' Correr went on to reveal appropriate republican sympathies. 'If the people submit to this present prejudice they are submitting to an eternal yoke and burying their past liberties which will remain a memory alone.' The Long Parliament put a stop to this eventuality though, as Christopher Hill reminds us, it was some little time before the people were brought into the proceedings and then only fleetingly.

England: some comparisons with France and the Dutch Republic

There can be no doubt that England, France and the Dutch Republic went through something amounting to a crisis in the mid-seventeenth century. But when we talk about 'crisis' do we mean the same thing in different states, which would suggest an underlying causal relationship, or different things in different states which would suggest that we can advance explanations internal and discrete to the respective countries? I am attempting no more here than to raise these issues for your consideration.

If we opt for the former view then we place ourselves alongside Hobsbawm and Trevor-Roper who link developments within these three states with general tendencies in western and central Europe at this time. If we take Hobsbawm's point, it is not perhaps unrealistic to see the crises in England and the Dutch Republic in terms of a clash between economic forces though, as J. H. Elliott has archly remarked, once we include France in this explanation, we cast the Frondeurs in the role of 'standard-bearers for a dynamic capitalist cause'! (Elliott, 'England and Europe: A Common Malady?') If we are attracted by Trevor-Roper's over-arching theory of a clash between 'Court and Country' on a European scale then we have to be convinced, say, that the French Court at the Louvre, which by extension had a standing army and a centralized bureaucracy, was the same as the English Court at Whitehall which possessed neither; and that, in particular, 'the aspirations of the Parliamentary opposition of 1640–42 were in fact anti–Court and decentralising in character'. (Stone, *The Causes of the English Revolution 1529–1642*, p 37.) If we take the view that 'crisis' was purely an internal matter for the respective European states, we need to be aware that we are turning our backs on what is now something of an orthodoxy, i.e. that the states of western and central Europe in the seventeenth century experienced a political and economic crisis of supra-national significance. We would also deny ourselves the insights into both national and European developments that can be obtained by comparative approaches, investigations and methods.

I would like to conclude by suggesting two different comparative bases for considering the significance of French and Dutch models of society. The first relates to the seventeenth-century context itself and raises questions about the way that English perceptions of French and Dutch experience influenced the course of events in England at that time.

The institution of monarchy can serve as one example. Compare Stuart subscription to the theory of Divine Right of Kings (see the Anthology, extract 10) with Bourbon deification. 'It should be recognised that over and above the universal consent given by peoples and nations the Prophets announce, the Apostles confirm and the Martyrs declare that Kings are ordained by God, and not only that but that they are indeed Gods.' (Assembly of the French Clergy 1625 cited in Prestwich 'The Making of Absolute Monarchy 1559–1683', p 112.) To what extent did the Stuarts take comfort from the Bourbons? How much influence did the style of the French court have on the English court? Did Charles I consciously attempt to build up a standing army and a centralized bureaucracy along French lines? Conversely to what extent did the example of French centralization stiffen the opposition among the English aristocracy and gentry to Stuart policies? These are just some of the intriguing comparative questions that occur under this head. Representative institutions provide another example. Did Dutch republicanism broaden the vision of the opponents of English monarchy? Did the existence of the Dutch States General act as a source of encouragement for those who attempted to resist the absolutist claims of the Stuarts? Did the moribund state of representative institutions in France serve as a warning to the English gentry?

The second comparative base takes a longer historical view and looks back at the events of the seventeenth century from the vantage point of present-day concerns about the nature and evolution of European society. From this perspective the following kinds of questions are raised. Did the seventeenth-century English experience constitute a crucial phase in the development of capitalism? Did the kind of societies that developed in France and England in the second half of the seventeenth century constitute fundamentally different types? How far can we accept Polišenský's view that the 'new pair of models represented by France and England were to set the tone of European life until the nineteenth century'? (Polišenský, *War and Society in Europe 1618–1648*, p 217.)

Irrespective of the way that we answer these sorts of question relating to the two different comparative approaches outlined above, I would suggest that our potential for understanding the explosive character of seventeenth-century English society is greater because they have been raised.

Politics in a Changing Society

The title of your set book, *The Century of Revolution*, shows that I think there were profound changes in seventeenth-century England. Not all historians agree; Charles Wilson, article 9 in the Reader, gives an alternative point of view. But, whatever words we use, we have to explain why there was a civil war in the middle of your period and the 'Glorious Revolution' in its last year. How does Lawrence Stone's analysis help us to understand these events? Any conclusions you arrive at now must be tentative: they may well have changed by the end of the course. But here is my view, which you might take as a working hypothesis, to be tested as you go along.

Reading 'England and Europe' will show you that a main problem is to decide why England did not follow France and most continental countries towards an absolute monarchy which either dispensed with representative assemblies or rendered them totally ineffective: whereas in England by the end of our period Parliament is the senior partner in government. The key words in the answer are those emphasized by Kevin Wilson in discussing French absolutism: taxation, armies, bureaucracy (p 60).

Unlike continental monarchs, the King of England could not raise taxes without the consent of the taxpayers through their representatives in Parliament. If you look at pp 38–47 of *C of R* (skipping the bits that relate to the period before 1618) you will see that Charles I tried to tax without Parliament's consent; but in the long run he failed. Why did he fail? He failed because he had no military force at his disposal to coerce unwilling taxpayers. Why not? Continental monarchies had built up permanent professional armies in the process of fighting wars which had become vastly more expensive as gunpowder replaced bows and arrows. Armies were essential to national defence, but they could also be used for internal repression – including the collection of taxes from reluctant payers. Britain is an island; national defence is consequently the affair of the navy, and navies cannot be used for internal repression. Could the Stuarts ever have made themselves financially independent unless they could build up a standing army? If you look at the Petition of Right in the Anthology (extract 13) you will see that one of its clauses concerns taxation without consent of Parliament, one concerns arbitrary imprisonment of those who refused to pay; the other two deal with martial law and billeting troops – i.e. with the government's attempt to get and keep an army.

Continental armies did not, of course, in fact collect taxes, except in the last resort: collection was done by the royal bureaucracy – permanent civil servants paid by and therefore dependent on the monarchy. By continental standards England had no effective bureaucracy. You could not pay tax-collectors until you had a permanent system of regular taxes to pay with. England was administered by unpaid officials, JPs, drawn from the gentry. Such military force as there was – the unpaid county levies, the militia – was officered and controlled by deputy lieutenants, drawn from the greater gentry. Taxes – even those not voted by Parliament – had to be assessed and collected by the gentry. So how could government be carried on in opposition to the gentry's wishes?

When we say that 'the JPs' did this, that and the other, they too lacked a subordinate bureaucracy. Just as the government depended on them, so they depended on unpaid subordinates – village constables, churchwardens, overseers of the poor. We have met these village officials before, men drawn largely from group 3A in our modification of Stone's analysis. As a group they were becoming richer and more independent. Most of them had votes in Parliamentary elections.

Traditionally, however much men grumbled, taxes were paid in time of war, even if they hadn't been voted by Parliament. But as the crisis described by Kevin Wilson developed, governments found it more and more difficult to pay their way, even in time of peace. In the 1620s – a time of economic depression and great poverty – war was almost continuous, as well as con-spicuously unsuccessful and unpopular in its objectives (*C of R*, pp 47–50 will give you more details).

Most of the gentry – and consequently the House of Commons – wanted to avoid conflict with the government. 'If there were not a King', James I had reminded JPs, 'they would be less cared for than other men'. The authority of 'the natural rulers' over their tenants and subordinates might be challenged too. The traditional hierarchical society was being subjected to unusual strains: none of those who benefited from it wanted it to collapse. Yet the gentlemen who sat in the Parliaments of the early Stuarts were very conscious that representative assemblies were ceasing to exist in most conti-nental countries; if they ever forgot it, Charles I and his ministers reminded them. MPs were responsible to those who elected them: strains in the society could hardly not be reflected in a growing restiveness among those who paid the taxes.

An excellent book by Derek Hirst, *Representative of the People?*, has shown that MPs were becoming subject to unprecedented pressure from the electorate – largely composed of group 3A again. MPs were caught between two millstones. How could they go on surrendering to royal demands for more and more taxes, enforced by arbitrary arrest, especially when it looked as though the government was aspiring to absolutism based on military force? Military absolutism would have taken away the natural rulers' author-ity over their localities even more than loss of the confidence of the electo-rate.

The government, on the other hand, trying to solve by traditional means the new financial problems with which it found itself faced, expected the co-operation of 'the natural rulers' when points had to be stretched a little. It had normally enjoyed their co-operation in the past. But now more and more points had to be stretched more and more often: this I hope is adequately illustrated in Chapter 4 of *C of R*.

The solution found by the end of our period was a transference of sovereignty from King to Parliament, the representative of the taxpayers. Once it has happened, this seems obvious common sense. But it took the experience of eleven years' personal government, civil war, regicide, republic, restoration and another revolution before the settlement of 1689 was arrived at.

So we certainly should not think of Parliament before 1640 as a revolutionary body aspiring to seize power by force. Nor should we think of James and Charles as systematically aiming at the abolition of Parliament and the substitution of military absolutism. Governments were facing new prob-lems; like Parliament, they expected to solve them by traditional methods. When that failed, men did not know what to do. They quarrelled with one another. Factions in the government tried to build up support in Parliament: we should think not so much of Parliament against the Crown as of one faction in the royal government against another. In 1624 the Duke of Buck-ingham and Prince Charles used Parliament to pressurize James into war with Spain. Soon afterwards, other factions in the government used Parlia-ment to impeach Buckingham himself.

This was a risky, not to say a desperate game. By 1629 consensus politics had broken down, and Charles I had to try to rule without Parlia-ment. As Kevin Wilson suggested, a breach opened up between 'court' and 'country' which was cultural and ideological as well as political. We shall be exploring some aspects of this in Block 2. In the 1630s the budget could be balanced only by virtually opting out of foreign affairs. The ultimate logic was to build up an army, as Wentworth was believed to be doing in Ireland, and a bureaucracy. The apparatus of the church and its system of courts, it might be suggested, were the nearest the Stuart monarchy ever got to a bureaucracy.

Here we come back to parish élites again. The church, no less than the state, had to rely on unpaid local officials to enforce its will, to present malefactors before its courts. Churchwardens were increasingly out of sympathy with the Laudian régime in the 1630s, increasingly unco-operative. In 1639–40, when the government was involved in war with Scotland, the system collapsed. (We shall discuss this in Block 3, *A Divided Society*.) To pay for the war a Parliament had to be summoned. When it met, the nether millstone proved harder than the upper: feeling in the country was so strong that MPs had to face the breach with the royal government that they had so long tried to avoid. They found themselves launched into unknown waters, in a vessel which proved difficult to control.

References

Ashton, Robert (1978) *The English Civil War*, Weidenfeld and Nicolson.

Bush, Douglas (ed.) (1976) *The Portable Milton*, Penguin. (Set book)

Clifton, Robin (1971) 'The Popular Fear of Catholics during the English Revolution' in *Past and Present*, No. 52, p 32.

Elliott, J. H. 'England and Europe: A Common Malady?' in Conrad Russell (ed.) (1973) *The Origins of the English Civil War*, Macmillan.

Hill, Christopher (1979) *Milton and the English Revolution*, Faber.

Hill, Christopher (1980, revised edition) *The Century of Revolution*, Nelson. (Set book)

Hirst, Derek (1975) *Representative of the People?*, Cambridge University Press.

Hirst, Derek (1978) 'Court, Country and Politics before 1629' in K. Sharpe (ed.) (1978) *Faction and Parliament*, Oxford University Press.

Hobsbawm, E. J. (1954) 'The Crisis of the Seventeenth Century' in T. Aston (ed.) (1965) *Crisis in Europe 1560–1660*, Routledge.

Hughes, Ann (ed.) (1980) *Seventeenth-Century England: A Changing Culture*, Vol 1 *Primary Sources*, Ward Lock. (Course Anthology)

Hunt, William (forthcoming) *The Puritan Moment: the Coming of Revolution 1570–1642*, Harvard University Press.

Kamen, Henry (1971) *The Iron Century: Social Change in Europe 1550–1660*, Weidenfeld and Nicolson.

Kenyon, J. P. (1978) *Stuart England*, Allen Lane.

Kossman, E. H. (1976) 'The Singularity of Absolutism' in R. Hatton (ed.) (1976) *Louis XIV and Absolutism*, Macmillan.

Lublinskaya, A. D. (1968) *French Absolutism: The Crucial Phase 1620–29*, Cambridge University Press.

Macfarlane, A. (1970) *The Family Life of Ralph Josselin: A Seventeenth-Century Clergyman*, Cambridge University Press.

Macfarlane, A. (ed.) (1976) *The Diary of Ralph Josselin, 1660–1683*, Oxford University Press.

Owens, W. R. (ed.) (1980) *Seventeenth-Century England: A Changing Culture*, Vol 2 *Modern Studies*, Ward Lock. (Course Reader)

Parker, G. and Smith, L. M. (1978) *The General Crisis of the Seventeenth Century*, Routledge.

Polisenský, J. V. (1978) *War and Society in Europe 1618–1648*, Cambridge University Press.

Prestwich, Menna 'The Making of Absolute Monarchy 1559–1683' in J. M. Wallace-Hadrill and J. McManners (eds.) (1957) *France: Government and Society*, Methuen.

Price, J. L. (1974) *Culture and Society in the Dutch Republic during the Seventeenth Century*, Batsford.

Rabb, T. K. (1975) *The Struggle for Stability in Early Modern Europe*, Oxford University Press.

Stone, Lawrence (1972) *The Causes of the English Revolution 1529–1642*, Routledge.

The Open University (1978) A101 *An Arts Foundation Course*, Units 6–8 *Introduction to Literature*, The Open University Press.

Trevor-Roper, H. R. (1959) 'The General Crisis of the Seventeenth Century' in T. Aston (ed.) (1965) *Crisis in Europe 1560–1660*, Routledge.

Wrightson, Keith and Levine, David (1979) *Poverty and Piety in an English Village: Terling, 1525–1700*, Academic Press.

Acknowledgements

The authors of Block 1 are grateful to Dr Rosemary O'Day for her preliminary draft 'Social and Economic History Background' which formed a basis for parts of this block.

We are also indebted to Dr William Hunt for permission to quote from his book *The Puritan Moment* before publication.

Seventeenth-century England: A Changing Culture, 1618–1689